# Edgar Cayce
## on
# Soul Mates

## Books by Kevin J. Todeschi

*The Edgar Cayce Ideals Workbook*
*Edgar Cayce on Soul Mates*
*Edgar Cayce on the Akashic Records*
*The Encyclopedia of Symbolism*
*Twelve Lessons in Personal Spirituality*

## A.R.E. Membership Series

*Edgar Cayce's ESP*
*Edgar Cayce on the Reincarnation of Famous People*
*Edgar Cayce on the Reincarnation of Biblical Characters*

# Edgar Cayce
## on
# Soul Mates

*Unlocking the
Dynamics of Soul Attraction*

Kevin J. Todeschi

ASSOCIATION FOR
RESEARCH AND
ENLIGHTENMENT

A.R.E. Press • Virginia Beach • Virginia

7th Printing, April 2003

Printed in the U.S.A.

A.R.E. Press
215 67th Street
Virginia Beach, VA 23451-2061


Library of Congress Cataloging-in-Publication Data
Todeschi, Kevin J.
    Edgar Cayce on soul mates : unlocking the dynamics of soul
attraction / Kevin J. Todeschi.
        p.    cm.
    ISBN 0-87604-415-1
    1. Soul mates.  2. Cayce, Edgar, 1877-1945—Edgar Cayce
readings.  I. Title.
BF1045.T58T63    1999
133.9—dc21                                                  98-45099

Cover design by Lightbourne Images

**To Mary,**

*My life partner, my teacher, my friend, my soul mate:
In appreciation of our interconnected learning journey
through time and space . . .*

# Contents

# Contents

# *Preface*

Soul mates. Even the words conjure up images of romance, candlelit evenings, laughter, moonlit walks, passionate embraces, unconditional love, and coming together as one. Such a relationship has often been perceived as one's "other half" who longs only to cling to oneself. It has been described as divine love made manifest in the earth. It is an individual's twin, a physical embodiment of one's spiritual complement. A soul mate relationship is the ultimate connection with another human being. It is the ideal union, portrayed to us by our peers, our parents, our teachers, our hopes, our stories, and our legends. It is a bond in which dreams are realized and one's selfhood is encouraged to blossom and grow—cultivated by the one we call "soul mate."

Who doesn't desire such a relationship?

For some, a soul mate relationship is one in which there are no challenges, no conflicts, no strife, only the opportunity to explore one another as equals, sharing joys, consoling sorrows, and being indivisible when united as one. Others, perhaps more realistic, see such a relationship not so much as an immediate reality but rather as a goal toward which they can grow. Regardless of whether it is seen as something created or something destined from birth, most individuals perceive a soul mate relationship as being preferable to "just a relationship." It is somehow superior to what others have settled for—oftentimes, even better than the kind of relationship in which an individual may currently be involved. After all, if more people had truly found their soul mates, wouldn't far less than half of all marriages end in divorce?

Just what is a soul mate? Where did the idea originate and why are we so fascinated by the topic? Although I had heard of the concept of soul mates previously, the first real discussion I had about the subject was nearly twenty years ago. At the time, a dear friend of mine surprised me with the news that she was divorcing her husband because she had found her "true soul mate." A beautiful woman, wife, and mother of two children, she confided to me that she didn't feel complete with her husband. For years, she had felt as if a piece of herself were missing. She was convinced that, at last, she had found her other half. Although not wanting to appear cynical, I couldn't help but think she had once felt the very same way about her husband, whom she was now divorcing. Maybe there was more going on in her situation than either of us was aware.

I remember wondering aloud whether or not there couldn't be more than one soul mate for each individual? If so, couldn't her husband be one of these, as well? If each of us only had one soul partner, what were the odds of ever finding one another in the first place? In the face of such an enormous planetary population, the prospect didn't appear very promising.

In the end, my friend followed through on her desire to leave her husband. The attraction she had toward this "soul mate" was overpowering. She divorced her husband, began the new relationship, and eventually moved to another state. Unfortunately, her "other half" relationship was not long in duration. In spite of the undeniable attraction between the two, troubles began almost immediately and her soul mate relationship came to an end within six months.

Since that time, the idea of every person possessing at least one soul mate somewhere in the world has grown in Western culture. Bestselling books by many individuals including Jess Stearn, Brian Weiss, Shirley MacLaine, Richard Bach, and Thomas Moore have gained widespread attention. Perhaps the notion of soul mates is inextricably linked to the concept of reincarnation, which has continually gained acceptance during this same period of time. But the idea of soul mates is not new. It has existed for thousands of years in many different cultures.

In both myth and legend, the original concept of soul mates appears to be that at some point in the ancient history of the world there occurred either a literal or a metaphorical division of humankind. Essentially, the idea is that the human soul was once whole and complete and somehow became separated or fragmented. Since that time, each individual has felt incomplete and now finds himself or herself searching for wholeness and his or her other half.

According to the Greek philosopher Plato (ca. 427-347 B.C.), humans are forever looking for their counterpart because they were once divided in half by the god Zeus. In *Symposium*, one of Plato's most famous dialogues, he states that the original human creation was somewhat different than at present. To begin with, there were three kinds of human creatures: men, women, and individuals who were of both sexes in one. In addition, each of these creatures had four legs, four arms, two faces, four ears, and two sets of genitalia.

Sometime after their creation, humans apparently

became arrogant and began to question whether or not humankind might take the place of the gods. Some even planned to climb toward the heavens and replace the gods with themselves. The idea put all of the heavens in an uproar, and all of the lesser gods debated with Zeus about what should be done. On the one hand, it would be relatively simple for the gods to destroy humankind; but on the other, the gods very much liked receiving offerings and tribute and if humanity ceased to exist, so would the devotion.

Finally, Zeus had an idea. He proposed cutting all humans in half. Not only would such an act cause the human creature to be only half as strong, but it would also double the number of humans—the gods would have even more individuals providing them with offerings and tribute. The plan was met with great enthusiasm by the gods, so each human was cut in half. The place where the two creatures had once been united was "closed up" and a new creature was formed, one with two legs, two arms, one face, two ears, and one set of genitals. The plan worked. However, in addition to stopping the human creature from supplanting the gods, Zeus's act had also left each individual with a deep longing for its other half. To help these human creatures find some solace, Zeus enabled each half to have intercourse with another half, thus creating one whole. Those creatures that had originally been only male would forever seek out another male with which to join. Those creatures that had originally been female would find comfort in the arms of another woman. And those creatures that had been both male and female would seek after its opposite sex half, enabling the species to propagate itself.

Although Plato's mythic account of humanity's division may appear far-fetched to some, it is not unique. A similar idea exists in Judeo-Christianity within the Old Testament. In the first chapter of Genesis, on the sixth day of Creation, God fashions a creature " . . . in his own image . . . male and female created he them" (Genesis 1:27). In its origin, God's creation seems to be androgynous, containing both sexes in one, and comprised of the essence of spirit. Not only are we told this creation is in the image of God (Spirit), but after the seventh day of Creation (when God rests), He suddenly realizes that "there was not a man to till the ground." Finally, God decides to make His spirit-creature "a living soul," by breathing into its nostrils the breath of life and Adam comes into physical existence. Afterward, the Creator does not want His human creature to be alone and He creates Adam's counterpart out of the man's rib:

> And the Lord God caused a deep sleep to fall upon Adam, and he slept: and he took one of his ribs, and closed up the flesh instead thereof;
> And the rib, which the Lord God had taken from man, made he a woman . . .
>
> Genesis 2:21

In the New Testament, Jesus reminds the Pharisees that God, during the Creation, had originally made them "male and female . . . For this cause shall a man leave father and mother, and shall cleave to his wife: and they twain shall be one flesh . . . no more twain, but one flesh" (Matthew 19:4-6). As in Plato's story, the human creature was once whole but was divided by the creation of its mate. These accounts have led some to believe that human beings are imperfect creatures and can only find some sense of wholeness—whether literal or psychological—as they are reunited through love, relationship, or marriage.

Apart from the Old Testament, several accounts of the creation of men and women exist in rabbinical literature. The Midrash states that God originally created Adam "two-faced" before deciding to cut him in half into the male and female creature. Elsewhere, it is suggested that Adam was originally androgynous and contained both sexes in one. A corresponding idea is found in Hinduism as the universal soul becomes conscious of itself, desires companionship, and, therefore, brings forth from its own Being the male and the female:

> In the beginning this was Self alone, in the shape of a person. He looking round saw nothing but his Self . . . But he felt no delight. He wished for a second. He was so large as man and wife together. He then made his Self fall in two, and thence arose husband and wife.
>
> Robert O. Ballou
> *The Portable World Bible*

Because the East and the West perceive wholeness as containing the polarities of male and female, yang and yin, anima and animus, many individuals contend that the human soul is ultimately androgynous and will eventually return to the same state. Regardless of the origin of this idea of a one-time division of human beings, it appears as though personal wholeness is achieved only through the process of having relationships with those who are external to oneself.

Perhaps the oldest written account of soul mates dates back approximately 5,000 years ago to the legend of the Egyptian gods Osiris and Isis. The story is one of eternal love in which the male and female deities are described as brother and sister as well as husband and wife. Destined to be together, Osiris and Isis begin their connection in the womb, where they are conceived together and from which they emerge as twins. From birth, each is beloved to the other. Their love is so strong and pure that even death cannot quench their feelings or ultimately tear them apart.

Because of envy and jealousy, Osiris is kidnapped and eventually killed by his brother, Set. In spite of Osiris's death, Isis is able to merge with her husband's spirit and conceives a god-child, Horus. Set is further angered and manages to have his brother's dead body cut into fourteen pieces. Although deep in mourning, Isis shows her eternal love by traveling throughout the country, gathering the pieces of her husband together and reassembling them until he eventually comes back to life. Her undying commitment to Osiris keeps their relationship alive. To the Egyptians, Isis was the goddess of fertility and motherhood, Osiris the god of the dead, and their offspring, Horus, the god of the sun and the sky.

Throughout history, humanity's search for wholeness has been depicted in myth, fairy tale, and legend. It is the consummate story of the prince's search for the woman who wears the glass slipper in *Cinderella*. It is that perfect kiss that brings one back to life in *Sleeping Beauty*. It is Beauty's love that causes the Beast to be transformed. It is the legends of frog-princes, the need for Romeos to be with Juliets, and Cupid's arrow causing an individual to change her or his direction; all reminding us that there is something incomplete about the lone human condition, so we find ourselves in search of wholeness.

There is no question that individuals are drawn toward one another, but what causes it? Is a chance meeting between two people simply accidental or is it destined? What motivates people to search for something they cannot quite define or have a sense of looking for someone that they've never even met? Is some undefinable impulse responsible for that inevitable intersection of lives which eventually brings two people together? Is it lawful and purposeful or is it random and unintentional? Is that something biological, emotional, or intellectual, or is it even more than we have perhaps allowed ourselves to imagine? Does fate play a role in our lives? Just what are the dynamics of soul mates and soul attraction and what effects do these forces have upon all individuals? Unique answers to questions like these can be found within the work of Edgar Cayce (1877-1945)— one of the truly remarkable men of the twentieth century.

In 1938, a fifty-eight-year-old woman came to Edgar Cayce to inquire about her life's direction. Cayce, considered to be the most documented clairvoyant of all time, had already assisted the woman with a health condition. A former schoolteacher and counselor, the woman had been married and divorced. Interested in the possibility of another relationship, she asked Cayce an insightful question that connected the concept of soul mates with her own search for wholeness. She inquired, "Please explain for me what is meant by 'soulmate' in relation to my own spiritual development." Cayce replied:

Those of any sect or group where there is the answering of one to another; as would be the tongue to the groove, the tenon to the mortise; or in any such where they are a complement one of another—that is what is meant by "soul-mate." Not that as from physical attraction, but from the mental and spiritual help. 1556-2[1]

From Cayce's perspective, the topic of soul mates was

---

[1]During Cayce's life, the Edgar Cayce readings were all numbered to provide confidentiality. The first set of numbers (e.g., "1556") refers to the individual or group for whom the reading was given. The second set of numbers (e.g. "2") refers to the number in the series from which the reading is taken. For example, (1556-2) identifies the reading as the second one given to the individual assigned #1556.

not one of simply a physical or a sexual attraction; instead, it was a relationship inextricably linked to an individual's own process of spiritual evolution and growth. That premise is explored in much of the Cayce material.

Regardless of his documented talents as an intuitive, at first glance we might wonder what kind of insights Cayce's information can provide on the topic of contemporary soul mates. After all, Edgar Cayce gave his last reading in 1944, long before much of the information on soul mate relationships even became available. And yet, because of the nature of his work and the questions asked of him by individuals much like ourselves, Cayce may be uniquely qualified as an expert resource on the subject.

Over a period of forty-three years, Edgar Cayce gave intuitive consultations, called "readings," to individuals from every religious background and all segments of society. In hundreds, if not thousands, of instances, Cayce further explored how personal relationships interconnect with a soul's spiritual development. In fact, one of the undergirding premises in the Cayce information is that we most often come to know ourselves through our relationships with other people. Whether it is through learning about love in the face of someone we hold dear or growing in patience through a lifetime of challenges, it is through our interactions with others that we become aware of our shortcomings and our abilities. It is through our personal encounters that we come to realize what we need to work on, as well as what it is we have with which to work. Cayce believed that it was also through the dynamics of our relationships that we grow in our awareness of our true identity and our ultimate connection to God.

Perhaps what is most unique about the Cayce information in regard to soul mates is that it also provides a thorough analysis of hundreds of relationships played out within the framework of reincarnation. For more than twenty years in nearly 2,000 "life readings," Cayce explored for individuals their spiritual development through various lives and their corresponding past-life connections to present-day relationships. For example, when inquiring about the past-life connection with his present-day wife, a thirty-five-year-old man was told, "Ye have been companions oft before—in distress and in exaltations" (2421-2).

From Cayce's perspective, a soul mate relationship is an ongoing connection with another individual that the soul picks up again in various times and places. From a source of information he called the "Akashic Records" or "the Book of Life," Edgar Cayce could view the development of relationships over time and describe how past-life influences and choices impacted the present. But more than simply providing individuals with some philosophical dissertation, his readings detailed practical advice and counsel that his clients were able to work with and apply. Taken together, the Cayce material on relationships constitutes one of the most significant sources of information on the dynamics of all kinds of human interactions, the purposefulness of our experiences with one another, and the very nature of the soul.

Perhaps because of the deeply ingrained desire to find a perfect partner, that "other half," or a special someone with whom to make our life complete, today there are various misperceptions about the nature of soul mates. For some, the concept of soul mates contained in the Edgar Cayce material may appear quite different than that which has been popularized by contemporary society. From Cayce's perspective, a soul mate is definitely not an individual's other half that somehow enables that person to become complete. We are attracted to another person at a soul level not because that person is our unique complement, but because by being with that individual we are somehow provided with an impetus to become whole ourselves.

Through an ongoing process of relationships, experiences, and various lifetimes, the soul finds itself involved in a curriculum of personal growth and development. It is true that the destiny of the soul is one of wholeness, just as suggested by the original story of Creation; however, Edgar Cayce believed that eventually every soul would become whole within itself. From this perspective, soul mates ultimately are those relationships that assist each individual in his or her spiritual development and the inevitable attainment of wholeness at the level of the soul.

Kevin J. Todeschi<br>
Virginia Beach, Virginia

# 1

## Soul Mates

Love is patient and kind; love is not jealous or boastful; it is not arrogant or rude. Love does not insist on its own way; it is not irritable or resentful; it does not rejoice at wrong, but rejoices in the right. Love bears all things, believes all things, hopes all things, endures all things . . . So faith, hope, love abide, these three; but the greatest of these is love.                    I Corinthians 13:4-7, 13

It was 1926 and she was a Broadway star. Only twenty-four, she already had been the female lead in a major production. Her role as the young duchess opposite Otis Skinner in *Sancho Panza* had resulted in critics and fans alike calling her "alluring." Her life as an actress appeared on a fast track. Her name was Rose,[2] and now that the production was coming to a close, she couldn't help but wonder what came next.

---

[2] For the most part, all names used within this volume have been changed to maintain confidentiality.

Even though she hadn't started out to be an actress, acting came easy to her. Because of her love of music, she originally had planned to be a violinist and had studied at the Chicago Musical College. But her drive to play music soon faded, and she decided to take drama lessons instead. Becoming an actress was easier to accomplish than she might have imagined. Rose seemed born to the stage. A producer saw her in her first college play and offered her the ingénue role in his touring stock company. New York followed the touring company, and she was immediately cast in a major production. Doors opened for her. To many, she seemed destined for superstardom. She should have been content, but she was not. After her role in *Sancho Panza*, none of the new parts seemed right for her. She wondered whether she should continue to devote her energies to the theatre or had the time come for her to marry? She was in love and the appeal of home and marriage sometimes seemed greater than her desire to be on stage.

It might have been unthinkable for some to imagine, but within a year Rose would forsake her career as an actress, settle down with a husband, and devote her life to him and raising a family. Her drive to be an actress had lessened at the same time that her desire to be with him had grown. Rose had found her soul mate and their coming together would forever change her life's direction.

Although she was young, already she had come to believe that there were no accidents. Life had a way of bringing situations and experiences together—call it a divine script that provided her with potential entrances and exits. Most often, her role was simply to watch and listen for her cues. A part in a Broadway production of *Laugh Clown Laugh* two years earlier than her role in *Sancho Panza* had led her to the current crossroads in her life. While in the play, she had met two individuals who would become important in her life's direction: one a drama critic and the other a thirty-two-year-old businessman.

During a break from rehearsals, she found herself waiting at the pier for a relative's ocean liner to dock. Attractive, outgoing, and friendly, Rose soon engaged in conversation with the tall, distinguished-looking gentleman waiting next to her. A discussion of pleasantries soon led to Rose's discovery that the man was interested in theater. She mentioned her small part in the production of *Laugh Clown Laugh*, starring Lionel Barrymore. The gentleman promised to see her performance. As it turned out, he was John Corbin, chief drama critic for the *New York Times*.

After one of the play's performances, Rose received a note backstage from another man named Bryant Goodman. Mutual friends had asked that he look her up. She found him engaging and invited him to join her and her sister for dinner. Although Bryant had seemed normal enough back at the theatre, during their dinner conversation he started talking about mysticism, past lives, and a psychic friend of his back in Dayton, Ohio, named Edgar Cayce. Although she loved discussions of religion and philosophy, up until that night Rose had never even heard of reincarnation and she wondered to herself, "What in the world have I picked up here?" Still, she and her sister found Bryant fascinating, even though she couldn't possibly believe every word he said.

Time passed, and after *Laugh Clown Laugh* closed, a complimentary letter about her performance from John Corbin opened the next set of doors and she was cast as the female lead in *Sancho Panza*. She continued to see Bryant. She felt drawn to him. He was interesting, a talented businessman, and fun to be around. However, she still couldn't bring herself to believe all that he talked about. Much of his conversation included wild tales of

this Edgar Cayce who reportedly could diagnose ill-
nesses while asleep as well as provide insightful business
advice (which Bryant claimed he relied heavily upon).
Bryant also believed that Cayce could somehow see how
the events and relationships of former lives had an ongoing influence upon the present. For Rose, none of
these tales were stories she relished discussing with her
family when she talked about the man she was seeing.

Eventually, the *Sancho Panza* company went on the
road and one of the cities on tour happened to be Dayton. At Bryant's insistence, Rose invited Edgar Cayce and
his wife, Gertrude, to see the play so that she could meet
them. As it turned out, the Cayces loved the play, and
Rose asked if she could watch Cayce's own work with his
psychic readings. The next day Rose witnessed her first
reading, given for a five-year-old child who was having
difficulties keeping any food down; for some reason the
child began to regurgitate after every meal. The little girl
was slowly starving to death. The doctors had tried everything they knew without success, so the parents had
finally turned to Edgar Cayce for help.

Just as had been described to her, Cayce put himself
to sleep on the couch. His wife gave him the suggestion
that he would be able to examine the child while in his
trance state. Told to "find" the little girl who was in the
house (although not in the same room with the adults),
it was not long before he began talking, opening with
"Yes, we have the body." As soon as he began speaking,
Edgar Cayce's secretary started writing down everything
he said.

Rose watched the process with a great deal of skepti-
cism. She couldn't believe that an individual could
somehow tune in to another person's physical problem
(let alone see something as far-fetched as a past life).
Still, the Cayces took their work very seriously and the
little girl's parents seemed to take his every word as gos-

pel. Edgar Cayce discussed what was wrong with the child and recommended such things as a complete change of diet, consisting chiefly of very ripe bananas, and some physical therapies. Although Rose had often heard about this man's work, seeing it firsthand made her feel a little ridiculous.

The longer she listened, the more irritated Rose became. This man wasn't a doctor; by all accounts he had never finished high school. He had made no physical examination of the child, nor did he plan to. Gertrude had stated that her husband had no medical background or training. At the very least, Rose felt that this man was practicing medicine without a license. What if he recommended something that would kill the child? The thought both alarmed and outraged her. Still, the group watched and listened to the sleeping Cayce without question.

When the reading was over, Rose left the house as courteously as she could. After all, she was an actress. However, she was mad at the Cayces and disgusted with Bryant for believing in the whole business. To her relief, a few weeks later she heard from the child's parents and was surprised to discover that their daughter had completely recovered. The little girl was finally able to keep down normal food; Cayce's reading had apparently been successful. It was for that reason that Rose began to wonder if Bryant had been right about Cayce after all.

By the spring of 1926, the cast of *Sancho Panza* was back in New York. Although a success, the tour was finished and the play was over. Rose was having a hard time finding her next role. Nothing seemed just right. She began to question what she wanted to do with acting. At the same time, Bryant had begun asking her to marry him. She loved him and was unmistakably drawn to him, but did she really want to forsake the theater for home and cooking and babies? Because of the demands of each possibility, it didn't appear to her that she could pursue both successfully. Sometimes the idea of marriage was appealing, but on other occasions nothing could have interested her less. At other times, the spotlight of the theatre was wonderful, and yet the satisfaction of it wasn't totally fulfilling or lasting. For the first time ever, Rose found that she didn't know what to do with her life.

In part, to help her with her direction, Bryant suggested a life reading from Edgar Cayce. By this time, supported with the backing of some very influential New York business people, the Cayces had moved to Virginia Beach to establish a hospital for his work. Having heard even more success stories of what this man was somehow able to accomplish, Rose agreed to the reading.

To make the business of the readings seem even more incredulous, Rose learned that her reading would be done while the Cayces were in Virginia Beach and she and Bryant remained in New York. Apparently, Edgar Cayce didn't even need to be in the same city with Rose in order to tune in to her.

When the reading finally came, she was amazed by its accuracy. Any remaining doubts she had about the man or his abilities quickly disappeared. She wrote the Cayces to tell them that the information was more than just helpful and interesting. Without knowing her life story or her current dilemma, somehow the sleeping Cayce had perfectly analyzed her character, feelings, and talents. Rose was very impressed. Immediately, she requested readings on behalf of other members of her family.

Rose's reading told her that she could make a success of herself in music, literature, art, the stage, or the home. Edgar Cayce briefly discussed lives she had lived in early America, England, Germany, the Holy Land, and Greece. She had developed her appreciation for music in Germany, where she had been a singer and close to a renowned composer. There, she had shared her love of music with many others. Her talent of acting had been best expressed during her lifetime in Greece when she had been of beautiful stature and had given the people much enjoyment in her various roles. Her love of philosophy was traced to Chaldea where she had once worked in the temples. From the same period, she had also developed an innate love for home and family. Repeatedly, Cayce explained how present-day talents and feelings could be traced to her former appearances in the earth.

Cayce told her that if she remained an actress, within the year she would again have a great new role that satisfied her outlet for expression. In fact, he assured her that her career would reach even greater heights somewhere between the ages of twenty-eight and thirty. He told her that she could also make a success of the home; however, at this point in her life, she could not excel in both directions. She needed to choose. He did not advise her on which direction to take, only that the choice needed to be made. Her attraction to Bryant was because of various connections they had experienced in the past. They had known each other in different roles in early America, England, and the Holy Land.

Later, Bryant obtained his own reading from Edgar Cayce. He asked what would be the result of a marriage between himself and Rose. Cayce replied, "What they make it!" To be more specific, Bryant asked: "Is this girl the type and quality of womanhood best suited to this man for a successful life?" The answer came: "May be made so in each. No one is suited exactly in the beginning, unless it has been fore-ordained through the ages of the mating of each." Again, Bryant tried to obtain the response he was looking for. He asked: "Will they be perfectly happy always . . . ?" Cayce stated:

No, they will not always be happy, but these may
be always made content. Contentment and happiness are different elements, but both are of the
mind—yet, physical conditions must exist between
each that these may be made compatible, or that
the mind may be brought to that position wherein
each may be content. 257-15

Finally, Bryant asked directly, "Is this the right girl he
should choose?" He was told that she was. Because of
their feelings for one another, as well as because of the
confirmation in the readings, Rose and Bryant married
on April 17, 1927.

On most occasions, Edgar Cayce would not specify
whether or not a certain individual was the appropriate
marriage partner. As was often the case, when a twenty-
five-year-old woman asked whether or not her boyfriend
was the man she was supposed to marry, Cayce replied,
"He would be *one* man to marry!" (3834-1). Another
woman asked, "Have I met the man I should marry?" She
was told, "You have met several you *can* marry!" (3180-
2). Apparently, we all have more than one soul mate—an
individual with whom we have been together previously
and could create a positive relationship in the present.
Later, Rose and Bryant learned that they had been married to various other individuals in the past as well; their
relationship with one another in the present was simply
one possibility. However, it was a possibility that gave
each the opportunity to be a helpmate to the other and
provide for the better development of both individuals.

When a woman asked about the possibility of marriage and meeting her soul mate, Cayce told her, "It is
not necessarily true that any special individual may be
called a mate, as there have been many . . . " (2487-2). On
another occasion, in 1942, a young woman wanted to
know if there was a person other than her fiancé whom

she might marry instead and be "as happy, or happier." She was told, " . . . we might find twenty-five or thirty such, if you chose to make it so! It is what you make it!" (1981-2). He went on to tell her that there were definitely some things from the past that needed to be "worked out" between herself and her husband-to-be and they might best be worked out in the structure provided by marriage. Sooner or later she would have to face these issues. Cayce advised her that she might as well face them now, rather than putting them off for some future time period.

A thirty-two-year-old sheet metal worker and his wife were having problems on and off again. During the course of their marriage, they had even discussed divorce and custody issues related to their child. In an effort to improve their relationship, the husband obtained a reading. The information made it clear that they had been together before, had failed, and were being given the opportunity to help one another succeed in the present. The man inquired, "What can I do to make our marriage happier and harmonious?" He was told:

> Act toward the wife, or thine own activities, as ye would like her or others to act toward thee. Ask no more than ye give. Demand no more than ye allowed, or allow, to be demanded of thee. Marriage, such an association, is a oneness of purpose. Unless there is the oneness of purpose, there can be no harmony. This can be accomplished, not of self alone—for remember, you made a mighty mess in the experience before this—ye suffered for it! Better make it up now or it'll be ten times worse the next time! 5001-1

From Cayce's perspective, the purpose of soul mates, marriage, or any lifelong commitment to another person is primarily to enable each individual to grow, to evolve, and to assist one another in spiritual development. To be sure, people are drawn together because of their joint experiences in the past, but what individuals do about those past-life experiences, an influence which Cayce equated to "karmic memory," is entirely dependent upon the activities and choices of the present. The readings suggest that each individual has multiple soul mates with whom she or he can make a successful relationship in the present. Obviously, each choice leads to different potentials and a lifetime of experiences, and some choices are ultimately better than others.

In 1940, in another example from the Cayce files (2205-3), a woman was acquainted with four different men, all of whom had expressed interest in being with her. A math teacher by profession, she wanted to know which of the four would make the best marriage candidate. She was told that it was incorrect to think that there was only ONE individual who would make her ideal mate. In fact, Cayce refused to tell her to keep away from this one or to be joined together with that one. Instead, he confirmed that in different periods in the earth she had previously been with all four of her suitors, "some as helpers, some as hinderers." He suggested that she needed to watch her dreams for they had provided her with "warnings" about some of the men. As to which choice to make in the present, she needed to decide for herself which one would better enable her to become a better person, to express a spiritual ideal, and to live a life of service.

The readings state that individuals are drawn to one another for a purposeful experience. Essentially, that purpose is both to resolve issues and challenges that were created in the past as well as to continue any positive interactions that were begun with one another. Good or bad, our relationships pick up exactly where we left them off. There is a continuity of former patterns, purposes, and ideals. The pull we may feel toward certain individuals in our lives occurs at the level of the soul and, according to Cayce, whether those former past-life experiences were for "weal or woe" does not prevent the present-day attraction. Ultimately, whether or not it is best for two individuals to elevate their attraction to a lifelong relationship should be based upon something greater than physical attraction and desire.

On numerous occasions, the Cayce readings advised an individual against getting married to a specific person. In spite of the attraction a couple might feel for one another, if marriage was discouraged, invariably the reason was because the union would not be best for the spiritual development of either or both individuals. In other instances, marriage was advised against because of timing issues. In one case in 1937, parents of a fourteen-year-old girl were told that their daughter would have the inclination to marry very early in life because she had been an old maid in her previous experience. The girl was encouraged not to follow through on her innate desire because it would become a disaster (1406-1). On other occasions, individuals were told not to marry until they had made a clearer choice about their life's direction. Apparently, each direction contained various possibilities of potential spouses.

A twenty-year-old woman asked whether or not she should marry her present boyfriend, and the response was "never" (1754-1). Cayce predicted that the relationship would inevitably lead to separation and divorce. He stated that she had known him in her most recent lifetime, during the American Revolution. At the time, around the area of Williamsburg, Virginia, the two had begun a relationship that had been both disappointing and happy at times. In the present, because there were some unresolved issues from the past, the woman felt an emotional desire to become even closer to him. The reading advised against it. Cayce warned, "It would be best *never* to marry him—thy ideals will be destroyed!" She was encouraged to maintain their friendship and to learn what they could from the other, but not to marry.

Since desire, attraction, and love might all originate at the level of the soul, how can individuals distinguish between a potential long-term relationship and one in which there is simply an attraction in order to work through something from the past? Cayce suggested that true love was ultimately best expressed as "giving in action," where one was not concerned with what was received in return. Whereas desire is a feeling or a condition in which an individual wants to draw someone or something to him- or herself, true love is an expression of emotion, energy, or activity that goes out to others without thought of what self receives in return. Ultimately, the purpose of all relationships is spiritual development. For that reason, individuals wishing to discern between a karmic relationship or a purposeful present-day union might ask themselves, "Does this relationship make me a better person? Does it challenge and stretch me? Does it encourage me to become a more balanced, giving person? Does this relationship bring out the very best within me?"

In 1937, a twenty-nine-year-old man asked Edgar Cayce to describe the best motives for marriage (1173-11). The reading stated that there was a vast difference between physical desire and mental/spiritual cooperation and companionship. If a marriage was based primarily upon desire and physical gratification, it could not succeed. Instead, a successful relationship had to contain a joint spiritual prompting that united the couple in service to one another as well as to God. Cayce believed that a healthy relationship included physical love, but it was much more; spiritual ideals and mental goals and aspirations were equally important.

Too often, individuals may believe there is one perfect soul mate that exists just for them. That is not the case. The condition of soul mates is also not limited to male-female relationships; soul mate relationships are just as likely to occur in same-sex relationships. More important, each of us has many different types of soul mate relationships. Some of those relationships might manifest in the present with various members of our family, friends with whom there is a deep bond and connection, and even work relationships in which individuals are brought together to achieve some greater goal. A soul mate is an individual to whom we are drawn in the present because we have been together in the past. It is a relationship in which each individual has the opportunity to be of invaluable assistance in terms of the other's personal growth.

Unfortunately, some individuals have mistakenly assumed that a soul mate relationship is a perfect relationship in which there are never any difficulties or challenges. They may then become frustrated because they haven't been able to find or create such a relationship in their own lives. The Cayce readings suggest that a soul mate will offer you problems and obstacles just as you will offer the same things in return. A soul mate is someone with whom you can work through life's challenges and difficulties, even when that individual may appear to be the source of them. In other words, a soul mate is an individual who often reflects or lets us encounter our own strengths and weaknesses.

By all accounts, Bryant and Rose had a very successful soul mate relationship, one that lasted over forty years—until Bryant's death in 1968. However, they also had their share of problems, arguments, and difficulties. Together, they experienced the normal ups and downs of any marriage. From the very beginning, they were burdened with the knowledge that Bryant's mother didn't like Rose as his choice for a spouse—the readings eventually traced the animosity to a past-life jealously and rivalry.

Within a few years of their marriage, Rose and Bryant would have two sons and obtain readings for each. They were told that the older boy had innate talents as a physician and the younger as a politician. When Bryant asked Cayce for advice in the boys' rearing and upbringing, it was stated that the most important thing wasn't power or might or even rules, but for him and Rose to live as an example to their children. The entire family had been brought together for a purposeful reason. Together, they could assist one another in fulfilling the purpose for which each had been born. In addition to the connections among the four of them in the past, they had the opportunity to become better people for having the experience of being brought together.

In spite of the fact that the readings had encouraged them to marry, throughout their life together, there would be challenges. Although financially successful, Bryant once told some friends that he had lost out on $500,000 by not following some of Cayce's business advice in the readings. World War II brought with it a series of shortages and difficulties, not to mention the fact that Rose, Bryant, and their children were Jewish at a time when prejudice was often common. Each of the children also had a series of problems, in addition to the normal events of childhood such as teething, colds, and sibling rivalry. The younger boy had scarlet fever, measles, anemia, and an accident in which he stuck himself in the right eye with a scissors and split the cornea. A series of readings and doctors saved his sight. The older boy had broken bones, chicken pox, measles, tonsillitis, pneumonia, and skin boils.

One of the couple's biggest challenges came when Rose began to miss the acting spotlight just as Bryant had become too focused on his business affairs. Understandably, Rose wanted more out of life than simply the roles of wife and mother. Because of her husband's financial status and business affairs, she often found herself an active part of society, which gave her some satisfaction. However, he was often out of town on business and rather than missing out on social functions, Rose allowed herself to be escorted by male friends. She saw nothing wrong with it. Bryant was quick to disagree. Arguments between the two could not be resolved. Finally, they obtained a reading.

Interestingly enough, years earlier Cayce had previously told the couple that as long as they worked together, they would each be able to bring out the best in the other and "gain for selves those developments that bring peace, joy, and happiness in a life worth being lived . . . " (903-3). They had been advised to always show their love for the other and to keep foremost in their minds their joint companionship. Rose's love of the spotlight would have to come second to their marriage, just as Bryant's focus on business matters and concerns could not be his first priority. Their home was to be their first and most important work. The two had been encouraged to keep their love alive, to find joy and peace in the other's company, to honor and to serve God, and to never make the same mistake with each other twice.

With the new reading, Cayce advised them that their most important activity was the raising of their children, especially during the boys' "formative years." They were reminded that their home was supposed to be their primary focus, and each was encouraged to renew within themselves that very attitude with which they had first established their lives together. Apparently, both Rose and Bryant had allowed themselves to forget the priority of their marriage. Rather than telling them specifically what to do, each was advised to again make their marriage come first. By working with one another, the problem was resolved.

In time, Rose became more interested in parapsychology and eventually sponsored lectures and programs that brought together leading scientists, scholars, and parapsychologists. In fact, for more than twenty years she put together a very successful lecture series in New York and acted as a catalyst for the study of metaphysics, yoga, and the Cayce work. She found in these efforts the limelight she had missed and helped many people by pulling the programs together. Bryant became even more successful in business and furniture manufacturing. For years, he also supported Temple Emanuel, the nation's largest synagogue, as well as the Cayce work. He and Rose had frequent opportunities to work together outside of their home, and many individuals saw their relationship as ideal. Their eldest son would become a leading psychiatrist and their youngest a successful attorney.

Rose lived to be in her nineties. A few years before her death, in reflecting back upon her family and the Cayce information, she said, "You notice not only the patterns and purposes of your own life, you become aware of how you are put into positions to assist others to carry out their activities." Soul mate relationships create an opportunity for personal growth, personal fulfillment, and service to one another.

In another example from 1940, a thirty-nine-year-old housewife, mother, and bookkeeper was told that she and her husband were making great strides in "meeting" and overcoming those shadows of patterns that had been created between them in the past. By working together, each was growing spiritually, each was developing, and their soul mate relationship was becoming even more positive. They were encouraged to continue as they were, for "each may be as a help, as a prop one for the other" (1857-2). Cayce told another couple that it would take them at least ten years to create an ideal relationship (cases 4159 and 459), but it could be theirs if they worked together.

A young couple contemplating marriage in 1942 was told that, as man and wife, they had the opportunity to be very helpful to one another. Apparently, they had been together many times previously in various relationship roles. During a lifetime in Persia, there had been conflict because the two had come together under false pretenses. In ancient Egypt, they had been raised with opposing belief systems, although they had learned to work together. As a result, in the present, Cayce told them, "They each, then, have that weakness of being able to be overpowered by the personality of the other." He advised them to cooperate with each other for the benefit of both, "Then if there is the agreement, if there is the coordination of ideals and purposes, and making same work—it can be made a beautiful companionship!" They were reminded, "It also can be made to be the belittling of one or the other" (1981-2).

A young New York lawyer obtained a reading about his pending marriage with his fiancée. He sought spiritual guidance, matrimonial happiness, and advice, which would enable the two of them to live successful lives. Cayce told the couple that as long as they kept their present feelings uppermost in their minds, they would be successful, "For their minds, their bodies, their desires, are in the present in accord." They were encouraged to remember that unison of purpose whenever dissension and strife arose in their marriage because compatibility and happiness needed to be created. It did not simply exist. They were told to become a complement one to the other. Cayce warned the couple that they would become divided in purpose if either became self-centered or gave in to selfish motives rather than remembering the importance of their relationship. From that day forward, they needed to learn to be able to depend upon the other. When the young man asked, "Do they genuinely love each other?" Cayce replied:

In the present. Remember each, love is giving; it is a growth. It may be cultivated or it may be seared. That of selflessness on the part of each is necessary. Remember, the union of body, mind and spirit in such as marriage should ever be not for the desire of self but as *one*. Love grows; love endures; love forgiveth; love understands; love keeps those things rather as opportunities that to others would become hardships.

Then, do not sit *still* and expect the other to do all the giving, nor all the forgiving; but make it rather as the unison and the purpose of each to be that which is a *complement* one to the other, ever. 939-1

Even as a young boy, Edgar Cayce had a recurring dream which seemed to suggest the importance of this "unison of purpose" in his own eventual marriage. In the dream, Edgar was walking through a glade with a woman standing next to him, holding his arm. The woman was wearing a veil so that he could not see her face, but they seemed very much in love. While walking, they arrived at a little stream filled with clear, sparkling water. They stepped over the stream and began walking up a hill where a man stopped to meet them. Dressed only in a loincloth, he was the color of bronze; on the man's feet and shoulders there were wings. He appeared to be Mercury, the messenger.

Mercury told the couple to join their hands, which they did. Across their united hands, the man placed a long piece of golden cloth and stated, "Together all can

be accomplished, alone nothing may be accomplished."
Suddenly, Mercury disappeared and Edgar and the
woman continued walking. Eventually, they came to a
road that was very muddy and the two wondered how
they would be able to cross it. In the midst of their confusion, Mercury appeared again and told them to join
hands and to use the golden cloth. They joined hands,
waved the cloth over the road, and immediately the mud
dried and the road became passable so that they could
continue on their journey. Next, Edgar Cayce and the
woman came to an enormous cliff that towered over
them. Using a knife, Edgar started cutting crevices in the
cliff for their feet and the two began to climb. Edgar
started up the cliff first, but he pulled the woman up after him. Hand-in-hand they ascended the rock. The
dream ended.

The first time the dream occurred was years before
Edgar met Gertrude, whom he married. At the time,
Edgar Cayce's mother apparently told her son that the
dream meant he would achieve a great deal when eventually united with his wife. Although he was married in
1903, the dream continued to occur. Finally, in 1926,
when Cayce had the dream again, a reading was obtained as to its meaning. The reading (294-62) stated that
the dream was apt to occur whenever challenges or significant changes occurred in his life. The dream was simply to remind him that he could face any challenge in
life or overcome any problem as long as he and Gertrude
were united, for "together all can be accomplished."

As soul mates, Edgar and Gertrude Cayce had been
together on a number of occasions in the past. According to the readings, a primary purpose for their lives this
time around was to focus their joint efforts into the psychic work that became Edgar Cayce's life calling. In fact,
it was suggested that the information obtained from his
psychic readings was very similar in scope to informa-

tion he had disseminated thousands of years previously during a lifetime in Egypt. While in Egypt, Edgar Cayce had been a high priest and Gertrude his wife and a priestess. At that time, Gertrude had acted as a spokesperson to the masses of people, even when her husband became too ill to perform his priestly duties. Apparently, the work they had begun together needed to continue.[3]

In this life, Edgar Cayce was also very dependent upon Gertrude. Before she took responsibility for conducting the readings, there had been occasions when he had been taken advantage of while in the psychic state. For example, individuals had done such things as stick a hat pin into his cheek to make certain he was really in a trance; others had requested health readings only to acquire betting tips for the horse races unbeknownst to Cayce while he was asleep. As long as his wife was present for a reading, Edgar Cayce felt confident that nothing could go wrong.

Both Cayce and his wife received frequent assistance in their own lives from the readings, as well. Gertrude was cured of tuberculosis and Edgar received relief from a digestion and elimination problem that affected him much of his life. Their lives together were dedicated to Cayce's psychic work. It wasn't easy because so much of the material seemed unusual. Although information on holistic health, reincarnation, dream interpretation, meditation, intuition, and the other subjects explored in the readings has gained acceptance and even validation today, at the time Cayce's work was not always accepted.

On the night before he died, Gladys Davis, Cayce's secretary, witnessed a final scene between the couple that so moved her, she made note of it in the Cayce archives (Case 294-8 Report File). Edgar Cayce was very weak and

---

[3]A further discussion of Edgar Cayce's past-life relationships with some of those closest to him is explored in the chapter "Twin Souls."

very ill. He was lying in his bed and his wife reached over to kiss him. What follows are Gladys's observations as she recalled the dialogue between Gertrude and Edgar:

> He said, "You know I love you, don't you?" She nodded, and he asked, "HOW do you know?"
>
> "Oh, I just know," she said, with her dear little smile.
>
> "I don't see how you can tell—but I do love you." Reflecting, he continued, "You know, when you love someone you sacrifice for 'em, and what have I ever sacrificed because I love you?"
>
> This bedside scene was so beautiful that it made Gladys cry . . . because she understood so well how Gertrude had stood by him and put his wishes always above her own when it came to the good of "the work."

What is perhaps most interesting about Gertrude and Edgar Cayce's commitment to one another is an experience that Cayce had in February 1941. Cayce's primary source of information for his psychic readings was the Akashic records—a collection of data that might be equated with the universe's supercomputer system. This collection of information, which Cayce also called "God's Book of Remembrance," keeps track of each individual's soul history, past lives, present experiences, and unfolding futures. While giving a reading, he had a dream in which he was looking through the Akashic records and saw what would have happened to him and his wife had they not gotten married. According to what he saw, "she would have died in 1906 of T.B. [tuberculosis]. I would have died in 1914 from a stomach trouble" (Case 294-196 Report File).

Edgar Cayce believed that all of our relationships with one another have the opportunity to become a purposeful experience. In the language of the readings, "They are *not* chance, but a divine purpose being worked out" (1722-1). Ultimately, that purpose is for the soul growth of all concerned. In terms of meeting a significant person or relationship in our lives, there are no accidents or chance encounters. Individuals are drawn together in the present because they have been together in the past. Nothing we learn from one another is ever forgotten just as every error we make with one another needs to be resolved.

Each of us is given a lifetime of opportunities to become a better person for having had the experience of all of our relationships. Whether or not those opportunities are fulfilled remains a matter of free will, but the potential is ever present.

As counselor, mentor, philosopher, and spiritual advisor, Edgar Cayce provided thousands of individuals with unique answers to questions regarding the dynamics of human relationships. From that body of information, it becomes clear that individuals are seekers, each in search of personal wholeness. Everything we draw toward us is simply the inevitable outcome of previous choices, decisions, and lessons learned—all leading to this particular event and moment in time. The Cayce material on soul mate relationships provides an extraordinary account of the continuous process of relationships through time and space and our various experiences and lifetimes in the earth. However, what may be most astonishing about the information is what it suggests about the nature of the soul, our relationship to one another, and the undeniable certainty that we are connected to our Creator in ways that the human family has yet to fathom.

# 2

## Soul Mate Case Histories

For even as love crowns you so shall he crucify you. Even as he is for your growth so is he for your pruning. Even as he ascends to your height and caresses your tenderest branches that quiver in the sun, so shall he descend to your roots and shake them in their clinging to the earth.

Kahlil Gibran
*The Prophet*

Just as is suggested by the old adage "when the student is ready, the teacher presents him- or herself," individuals are drawn together in the right timing, for a purposeful reason, sometimes almost in spite of themselves. In one contemporary example, a thirty-six-year-old Japanese male named Toby had sworn off marriage after having been through a very difficult first marriage and divorce. Instead of pursuing any permanent relationship, he found contentment in his work as a translator. Intelligent, dedicated to his company, and committed to the work he was doing, Toby's long work hours and changing schedule did not leave time for many social engagements, let alone dating.

At the same time, Asako, a female songwriter and novelist, had almost given up any hope of finding a mate. Although she was very successful, at thirty-five Asako had never married nor had she found any likely prospects. To many in Japanese society, she was fast becoming an old maid. As "chance" would have it, mutual friends toward year-end arranged a meeting of the two at a party.

It was one of the few parties that Toby had attended that year. The meeting between the two went well enough. He found Asako attractive, charming, and intelligent. However, when friends informed him of the level of her success, Toby put any ideas of a relationship out of his head. He considered himself poor by comparison. He had also sworn off relationships and had promised himself that he would not remarry, so the whole idea was an "impossible match," not to mention the fact that he felt "she was beyond my reach." For her own part, Asako felt that he was a pleasant enough person but did not see much beyond Toby "being a friend of mine." Apparently, each of their souls had something quite different in mind.

On January 1 of the New Year, both Toby and Asako were awakened in their own homes by a dream that seemed important. Each thought the dream was meaningful because in Japan the first dream of a New Year is considered to be very significant. Since Toby's dream seemed to concern Asako, he called her to tell her what he had seen. To his amazement, he found that she had just awakened from an almost identical experience. At the very least, the two were convinced that they shared some type of "strong spiritual connection." According to Toby:

In the dream, I took her to my parents' home in Japan. In real life, the house is a small, typical Japanese-style house, but in the dream it appeared to be a mansion. At first I showed her the bathroom, then the laundry room, and finally several guest rooms. To my surprise, she had a nearly identical dream. In her dream, some unknown man took her to a Japanese-style mansion. At first she was shown the bathroom, and then the washing machine, and finally she was taken to a large guest room.

Because of the dream and in spite of their initial thoughts to the contrary, the two decided to continue seeing each other. Within a few months they were married, and within two years of their meeting, they had a baby daughter. According to Toby, although their marriage occurred relatively soon following their meeting, after each had overcome their reluctance to come together, it felt "as if we had known each other a very long time." And, according to Asako, it was the strangest and most unexpected feeling as if "he might be the other half of my soul."

In an example from the Edgar Cayce material, a young man named Hans was ready to commit to a marriage relationship almost immediately, whereas Katherine, the young woman he was pursuing, appeared to be much more hesitant.

Hans worked for a very large Danish international trading company. Born in Denmark in 1914, he had transferred to the United States in 1936 and had become branch manager of the Seattle office in 1943. As Danish consul, he met Katherine in May 1943 and, in his own words, "a spark caught fire."

Katherine was born in Massachusetts in 1917. After graduating from interior decorating school in New York, she and her aunt (who raised her) were visiting friends

in Seattle. During their visit, Pearl Harbor was attacked
and the two were "stuck" in Seattle. Gas was immediately
rationed and there was no way to acquire the necessary
fuel to drive back east. Katherine and her aunt began
making new lives for themselves in Seattle.

Katherine became president of a young adult group at
the Congregational Church and invited Hans to come
speak. As Danish consul, he was willing to come to any
group and discuss "Denmark under the Nazi heel." All
arrangements were handled by phone. She met him at
the door to the church, where the meeting was to be
held. As soon as Hans reached out and touched her
hand, he noticed, "something happened within me and
I knew that I would have to see her again." He pursued
her from that moment on. At the time, he was twenty-
nine; she was twenty-six.

Katherine, however, was not interested in a relationship with Hans beyond friendship. She was seeing Richard, another young man who shared many of her interests,
but she didn't feel drawn to the idea of a permanent relationship with him either. She liked having friends, but
marriage seemed another matter. Katherine's Aunt Betty
had obtained a life reading for her niece previously in
which the two women were told that because of past experiences, Katherine was innately torn between a desire
to be loved and her desire to remain free.

In her most recent lifetime, Katherine, in terms of her
personal talents, apparently had been skilled with weaving, design, and needlework. In Rome, she had been involved with directing activities for various groups of
people. From that, she had developed a great love for the
outdoors, games, and sports. In Persia, she had also ex-
ercised an influence upon many people and representa-
tives of various nations. At the same time, she had also
worked with weaving, brocades, and silk. In ancient
Egypt, she had worked in the temples, assisting individu-

als in discovering their purpose in life. Most of her past lives, however, seemed to involve something to do with decorating and design. It was information that fascinated Katherine because she had specialized in textile design and decorating in the present and had won a scholarship to decorating school—information with which Cayce was not familiar at the time of the reading.

Aunt Betty became a good personal friend of Edgar Cayce. In 1943 she wrote to tell him of the two men who seemed interested in her niece and of Katherine's reluctance to commit to a relationship. Betty told him, "The two boys are thoughtful, spiritually minded, lovers of nature, etc., very much alike in SO many ways—both will be ideal husbands to whomever they may marry." In referring to Hans, she added:

> I thought he was NOT serious—but that is not the case. He is very much in love with Katherine—in fact, he proposed to her and she refused him. In hurting him, her own EMOTIONS have been aroused (for the first time) and Hans has decided that he spoke too quickly and he is willing to wait—with the hope that he can change her mind. He is being transferred to San Francisco . . . and he's hoping that Katherine will follow him by the New Year.
>
> Katherine has written Richard about Hans—of their outings together—riding, swimming, etc., and suddenly, in his letters, you begin to feel that he is getting worried. But he does not express his own feelings for Katherine and she feels that he has only a deep feeling of friendship for her.

In terms of Katherine's feelings for Hans, she saw their relationship as just a natural friendship. Although she enjoyed being with him—hiking, horseback riding, or simply having a conversation—she was not interested in

marriage. Hans would have to be content with a friendship that shared a love of the outdoors, a similar philosophical outlook on life, and a joint interest in spirituality.
In January 1944, Aunt Betty's letter to the Cayces provided an update:

> Hans has been transferred . . . He is such a fine
> boy, and so in love with Katherine. There must be
> some reason why she doesn't respond—for as far as
> I can see, he would bring great happiness to her.
> Perhaps she is unaware of what "Love" really is. Poor
> Richard . . . he is so despondent—we wish that he
> would consent to a reading, but in his present men-
> tal state, no one or nothing seems to reach him. It's
> really very sad . . . Of course, Katherine is disturbed
> and has tried to write him the sort of letters which
> would encourage him to rise above this mental de-
> pression. But it seems hopeless at the moment at
> least. Case 1770-8 Report File

Because of their interest in the Cayce work, Katherine
and Betty loaned Hans the Cayce biography, *There Is a
River*. After reading it, Hans became convinced that he
had met Katherine before, "in the long ago." As a result,
he requested a life reading. Because of Edgar Cayce's
busy schedule, the reading could not be scheduled until
April 1944. Aunt Betty looked forward to the reading as
much as Hans did because she believed that "a reading
might release Katherine in analyzing her own true feelings."
When April finally arrived, the reading confirmed that
Hans had many talents. His life was destined to include
much travel, international relations, trade, and diplomatic
initiatives. He was told that he was very intelligent and
was capable of being entrusted with great responsibility,
important relationships, and was innately a skilled leader:

For the entity has lived so as to be entrusted with and capable of directing the affairs of great organizations, corporations, states or nations. Then if the entity chooses spiritual and mental ideals . . . little should prevent the entity from making this material experience a light and a help to others as well as bringing harmony, peace and development spiritually and mentally in this particular sojourn. 4053-1

In his lifetime immediately previous to the present, Hans had been involved in the shipping trade between Denmark and the United States. In Persia, he had been a director of trade for goods traveling between Egypt and the Gobi. In ancient Egypt, he had been chosen by the government to be a representative of the country. In addition to other lifetimes when they had obviously known one another, it was in Persia that Katherine had become his wife. She had been his friend, his companion, and his trusted advisor to whom he often looked for guidance and counsel.

Hans was told that he would always hold his companion in awe and reverence. Cayce stated that it would be a good idea for Katherine and Hans to marry in the present and continue the relationship they had once shared in Persia. Apparently much had not been completed in their previous experiences with one another. According to Hans, he believed it was because of the advice given in the reading that finally, "Katherine surrendered and we were married in October 1944."

After their marriage Hans became commercial attaché and helped his country with the procurement of large quantities of urgently needed commodities, such as fuel and fertilizer. In 1947, when Denmark obtained a $40-million loan from the International Bank for reconstruction and development, Hans was chosen as the contact between Denmark and the International Bank and was authorized to withdraw and disburse funds from the loan. After the war and the reconstruction initiative of the Marshall Plan, Denmark received about $280 million in economic assistance between 1948 and 1953. Hans negotiated the programming of these funds and supervised all financial aspects of their procurement. At the end of 1953, he changed jobs and became U.S. representative for the Danish meatpacking industry.

He once stated, "My business called for me to travel abroad extensively; throughout, Katherine trusted me without any doubt—and I responded in kind. And [each] coming home was like another honeymoon."

In the 1950s Hans wrote: "I regard my vocation as an agency through which I can better fulfill my purpose in life. It is not just a place where I get the wherewithal to buy my house and feed my family, but a place in which I can express my purpose . . . " In 1964, he was knighted by Denmark for outstanding service to the Danish meatpacking industry.

Over the years Katherine and Hans provided updates to the Edgar Cayce Foundation regarding their life together. In 1998, after more than fifty years of marriage, Katherine wrote: "We are so in tune with one another. I think we've had many lifetimes together during which we rubbed off the rough corners, for this lifetime together has been a smooth sail." Of course, the couple had their share of difficulties; she added, "One doesn't have four children and not have challenges." Those challenges included a son's attempted suicide and his disclosure of homosexuality and their daughter's falling in love and wanting to marry a man of a different race, both situations occurring at a time when society frowned upon such relationships. For their own part, however, Hans and Katherine met all challenges "with support for each other, support for the child, applying our spiritual beliefs, and working with such things as forgiveness and acceptance. We sustained each other through challenges with prayer and trust."

Looking back on their marriage, Hans stated: "Our life together has been harmonious and wonderful. We have always supported each other throughout and have never had a fight." To be sure, differences of opinion have occurred, "but these are expressed reasonably and courteously." In regard to the children, "We always presented a united front. The children quickly learned that they could not pit one of us against the other. Their efforts to divide us were met with, 'What did Mom/Dad say?—that's the answer.'"

Their life together has been a joint effort of children, home, travel, and a commitment to a spiritual path in which each is in tune with the other. From Hans, Katherine has learned "to be less rigid—not seeing everything so cut and dried, black and white. I've become freer—more able to play and get out from under my puritanical ethic of responsibility." She feels as though he's also helped her obtain more balance in her life. From Katherine, Hans has learned "patience, the importance of color and design, a deep sense of caring. We showed each other trust and loyalty. Katherine learned Danish—which she has used widely in our visits to Denmark, and I backed her artistic abilities and encouraged her."

Repeatedly in their travels together, people who have just met them have commented about their relationship: "It's wonderful to see a couple so in love after so many years"; "You're both a delight—an inspiration for us"; "What a great example you two are"; and "It just feels good to be together with you two."

To sum it up, Hans says, "Our life together through fifty-four years—as of this moment—is a continuous story of love and understanding and faith." As to the formula for creating a successful relationship? "Give sixty percent and expect forty percent." Katherine adds, "Ac-

cept and overlook the small, picky habits, and appreciate the depth and warmth of love that outweighs everything
else."

A less successful account of soul mates is told in the
story of Anna and Dave Mitchell. In 1935, a twenty-eight-
year-old writer named Dave asked for a reading regarding the possibility of marrying his sweetheart of six years.
In the reading Cayce confirmed that the couple had been
together three times previously and in the present could
accomplish a great deal, "if their efforts are put in the
right direction" (849-12). Cayce stated that the two had
much to work out together, but it could be accomplished
"in patience, in tolerance, in love." Apparently, at a soul
level, they shared a dependency and a responsibility toward one another. At various times in the past, there had
been occasions when the two had both assisted and
been detrimental to the other's growth. In the present,
Anna and Dave were advised to marry and to always
keep foremost in their minds the fact that marriage was
a "fifty-fifty" proposition and that they needed to maintain a unity of purpose. Toward the end of the reading,
Cayce added, "Beware then, in *each*, of self and *self's* interest irrespective of the other."

Less than two weeks after their marriage, Dave sent a
letter thanking Edgar Cayce for his help:

> We are, of course, deliriously happy, and among
> other things we both want to thank you for that
> reading—it isn't going to be all a bed of roses, but
> with the knowledge and help that comes from your
> gift we hope that we can "take it" and keep going . . .

Over the years, Dave and his wife received a number
of readings about their relationship, Dave's career as a
writer, their past lives, and even readings for their baby
daughter who was born within two years of their mar-

riage. In one reading, the couple was told that the greatest influences affecting them from the past came from their joint experiences in England and ancient Egypt. In Egypt, the state had apparently chosen Anna to be Dave's wife—a situation that he rebelled against. It wasn't so much that he disliked Anna as it was he found repugnant the fact that the nation had such control over the affairs of its people. Obviously, Anna had felt abandoned by her husband's refusal of her.

In their most recent experience together in England, Dave had been a Catholic priest and Anna a nun. At the time, the two had been attracted to one another. Apparently, the priest had mentally dominated the nun and persuaded her to break their vows of celibacy against her better judgment. Anna had yet to forgive Dave for what had happened. Interestingly enough, in their present lifetime both Anna and Dave had been raised strict Catholics. However, the difference between the two was that Anna was very committed to her faith whereas Dave was almost hostile toward his. In spite of the antagonistic past-life influences between the two, Anna was told in her reading that if she worked on her personal relationship with Dave, she had the opportunity to "bring the greater satisfaction, the greater understanding, the greater blessings for self and for others" (1102-1). At the same time, Dave was told to put his energies into the importance of home and family.

In spite of their six-year love affair, shortly after their marriage differences between the two seemed to undermine the relationship. Anna grew more and more distressed about Dave's "revolt" from Catholicism. Dave stated he was convinced that "Anna will not be satisfied until I fully re-embrace the Catholic faith"—an event which he did not perceive as very likely. Perhaps because of breaking her vow of celibacy in England and because of being rejected in Egypt, Anna did not have the same desire for sexual frequency as did her husband. As a result, Dave called his wife frigid and Anna thought her husband's view of women both archaic and primitive. In the present, Dave also tried to dominate his wife mentally, just as he had done in the past. However, somewhere along the way, Anna had acquired a greater degree of independence and self-reliance. Rather than working together and resolving their differences, Dave became all the more focused on his intellectual pursuits and writing career and Anna became more distant. Each began to resent the other.

Within two years of their marriage, Dave was stricken with a crippling disease which, according to the doctors, resembled a combination of "arthritis, spinal meningitis, and infantile paralysis." Within a very short period of time, Dave was crippled to such an extent that he had some mobility only of his arms and was incapable of doing much of anything to help himself. As if to enable them both to rectify the broken vows of celibacy, sexual activity between the two was out of the question. Both individuals became miserable. Anna refused to divorce him because of her faith, and Dave told friends that marriage was so repugnant to him that if the time ever came when he was single and another woman tried to get him to marry her, "probably I would kill her." To Dave, the idea of being married to anybody was unthinkable. He added, "I feel wonderfully convinced that monastic life is the only approach to genuine happiness." Rather than working together or trying to resolve any of their differences, each remained steadfast in the opinion that it was the other who needed to change.

Because of his illness, Dave confined himself to such places as the Hospital for Joint Disease and Johns Hopkins. Although Anna felt obligated to visit him during his confinement, he did not look forward to seeing her, nor did he have any desire to return home. In spite of their separation, he continued to write to support his family, but was limited by his doctor to sit at his typewriter only an hour a day. In order to make the best use of his time, Dave composed and edited 1,000 words of copy in his mind before writing it out in the allotted hour. The pain of his illness was excruciating. Confined to a wheelchair, he underwent many experimental treatments, not to mention a reliance on such medications as aspirin, codeine, cortisone, nepenthe, various narcotics, and in his words "brandy."

Eventually, events in their lives necessitated Dave returning to live with his wife just as a stroke and paralysis struck Anna's father. As a result, Anna had two invalids—her husband and her father—to care for. Dave found the situation intolerable. In 1941, he obtained another reading and asked about how he was supposed to work with his wife. He was told, in part:

> For, they are necessary one to the other in filling those purposes for which their activities are in this present experience.
>
> As to application, this must be according to the choice of each. They *should* be cooperative, one with another. The *way* ye know. The application *ye* must make. 849-60

A few months earlier, Cayce had also told Anna, "Each needs the other" (1102-5).

Over the next ten years, Dave experienced repeated improvements and just as many relapses. In spite of his crippling disease, friends made it possible for him to make a number of trips, both for his treatment as well as for his writing career. Somehow, he was even able to travel to the Middle East in 1949 and write an eyewitness account of the new state of Israel. In all, during the time of his illness, he was able to write seven books, countless book reviews, and various magazine articles. He seemed happiest when he was away from home and kept busy with something he was writing. Anna, on the other hand, seemed happiest with their daughter.

Finally, in the midst of one of Dave's relapses and another one of the couple's reconciliations, doctors suggested a series of experimental operations to help Dave with his pain. From the very beginning, Anna was against the idea. However, Dave insisted that he wanted the treatment. After one of the operations, complications caused Dave's kidneys to fail and he died in January 1953. Dave Mitchell was only forty-five years old. In spite of the advice from the Cayce readings and a number of situations which seemed to almost encourage their need to work together, it doesn't appear as though Dave and Anna entirely overcame, healed, or worked through their soul mate experiences from the past. Inevitably, at some point in the future, they will have to come together again and work through the very same lessons.

Rather than demonstrating that a couple needs to have a life reading from Edgar Cayce in order to glimpse possible experiences from the past, the contemporary story of Mary and Brian suggests that both dreams and personal intuition can be just as significant. In January 1988, Mary moved to a medium-sized university town to begin a new life with her daughter, Nancy. Only thirty-six, she had been widowed a number of years previously when her first husband died of cancer. Mary decided to take a few university classes, find a new job, and start all over. The very night of her arrival she saw Brian in one of her classes and immediately sensed that "I had known him before." Later, she discovered that Brian was two years older than she was and had recently left the ministry in order to start a new life in the same university town. She recalls seeing him, as follows:

I felt as if I knew him from somewhere and was instantly attracted to him. I knew that I would be getting to know him better. I was not particularly pleased about this because having just arrived that morning I had a number of things I needed to do to get settled before I would have the time to explore or get to know people. I didn't want to take the time and couldn't afford the energy at that particular moment. I was more concerned with getting into my house, finding a job and getting my daughter settled in school.

A short time later, Mary had a dream that seemed to suggest she would be getting involved in a relationship after all. In the dream, she was going to some kind of gathering with a group of people. A couple she knew entered the meeting room with her, and the three sat together. Next to Mary, there was an empty chair. In the dream, she realized she was saving it for someone. Several times different people tried to sit in the chair, but Mary told them that the chair was taken. At some point during the gathering, Mary got up from her seat to have a conversation with a woman whose talent was dream interpretation. The woman told her that she, herself, had once had a precognitive dream in which the woman had met her own husband. During the course of their conversation, the woman and Mary discussed an old Victorian desk that had lots of hidden drawers in it. In one of the drawers, the two found a map of the United States. Mary remembered that the Mississippi River was clearly marked on the map and the woman pointed to a place right next to the Mississippi in the northern part of the country and indicated that what Mary was looking for could be found in that area. Mary thanked the woman and went back to her seat in the gathering room. As she went back to her seat, she realized that a man was now

sitting in the empty chair. She didn't know his name, but
the two of them and the couple with whom she had
come to the meeting began having refreshments together.

A couple of days later, Mary and Brian happened to
meet outside the university and decided to go out to
lunch. During their conversation, Brian mentioned that
he had been born in the northern part of the country, in
a small town next to the Mississippi. Over the next few
weeks, Mary started to get the impression that she and
Brian had actually been together in Victorian England.
She also sensed that Brian and she had been together
before England as well, during a lifetime when he had
been her son.

The two of them began dating; however, all was not
smooth along the way. In addition to Mary's daughter,
Nancy, not approving of the relationship, the couple had
a number of arguments. After one major disagreement,
the two decided not to see each other again. Their separation lasted only a few days.

As time passed, Mary began to get the sense that they
were picking up a relationship they had begun in England in the 1800s. At the time, she believed the two of
them had been having an affair. In her mind, she imagined that Brian had been a minister and had promised
to leave his wife, sail to America, and start a new life with
Mary's seventeenth-century self. However, Brian never
showed up and Mary waited at the docks in vain. During
that experience, Mary believed that Brian had been
about thirty-nine—his identical age to their meeting in
the present. Interestingly enough, when Brian later obtained a psychic consultation about a project he was
working on, the psychic unknowingly confirmed some
of Mary's past-life "imaginative impressions." What may
be just as interesting is the fact that, in this life, Brian
had been hopelessly drawn to a woman he could not

have because she was already married to another man. Both Brian and Mary felt as though the woman was the reincarnation of the wife he had been unfaithful to in England.

A year after their initial meeting, Brian and Mary moved in together and began their "lifelong relationship." Almost immediately, Mary's daughter, Nancy, began to do "almost everything she could" to get the couple to separate. According to Mary:

> Nancy tried to consistently drag him into power struggles with the hopes that Brian would either leave or I would choose her over him. Rather than falling into her trap, he sidestepped her. He never made me feel I had to side with him or choose him over her but encouraged me to have my own relationship with her. He helped me to see her side of the struggle and was always ready to listen and be supportive of my decisions. He never tried to get me to handle Nancy his way. By staying in the background and not forcing anything, he was able to help me help her. He didn't take her on directly which would have been devastating because she is very rebellious and would have come at him with a lot of anger and hostility. He has been very supportive of her and over the years she has grown to appreciate and love him. I am not sure of the karmic relationship among the three of us but I am sure it must have been some strong tie. The two of us together have tried to consciously meet it with love and understanding although not always successfully. Our greatest assistance in this endeavor has been our shared spiritual values, beliefs, and life philosophy.

Today, ten years after coming together, both Brian and

Mary feel as though their relationship is stronger than ever before. As a couple they have traveled to England, Scotland, Egypt, and Greece—places where the two are convinced they have been together previously. Both feel as though they were compelled to move to the university town in order to meet. And each is convinced that "if we had met any earlier in our lives we would not have gotten together. We both needed to grow and come to some point in our own growth to be able to handle the conflicts, demands, and growth opportunities that this relationship has afforded us."

From Mary, Brian has learned to open up emotionally and to feel comfortable expressing his feelings—something he shied away from previously. From watching Mary work with Nancy, he has also learned "what unconditional, persistent love is all about." Mary sees Brian as more accepting of others and capable of overlooking their weaknesses. "From him I have learned not to be so negative and condemning of others but to see them as humans who are trying to grow and support them in this endeavor." Each has given a sense of balance to the other's life.

According to Brian, their work as a couple is an ongoing process:

> I think the sense of unconditional love has grown as we have seen darker, more abrasive, more unpleasant sides of each other. In spite of learning about and experiencing these aspects of each other, there exists between us a love and acceptance of these parts as being necessary to the wholeness of whom each of us is at the moment. It is an acknowledgment that we are on the road to spiritual and emotional growth and that we are not there yet.

Mary believes that her relationship with her first husband was also a "soul mate" relationship, although different than the relationship she shares with Brian:

> I believe that my relationship with my first husband was also a soul mate relationship. We helped each other to grow on many levels. I helped him to face his illness and eventual death and all the struggles along the way. He helped me to learn what it was like to help someone face tragedy on a physical, emotional, and spiritual level. He also taught me how to give willingly to someone else and put his or her needs before my own. I was forced to grow as an individual after his death because I was left alone and had to learn how to meet that, grow through it, and flourish.
>
> Conversely, I was kind of lost in the relationship. I never had a sense of my own individuality, my own purpose or my own strengths and weaknesses. I totally and completely identified with my husband and blended into him. When he died, I was devastated and spent years defining who I was and growing as an individual. If I hadn't been able to achieve this growth, I don't think that my relationship with Brian would have survived. Brian hates clinging-vine types. Although he is quiet, he very much knows what he wants to do and who he is. I can put just so many demands on his time without him totally revolting. He then just becomes quieter, more separate, and retreats into himself. This reaction is the total opposite of what I want or need to feel connected to him. In order to give him the freedom and space he needs in this relationship, I have had to learn to have my own interests and be my own person. Where my first husband encouraged and loved the dependent person that I was, Brian would feel smothered by it. Most people who know me think

that I am a very dominant strong-willed person. I have become that over the years, but it is not my innate nature and there is always a part of me that wants to retreat into someone else. Brian has encouraged my individual nature.

Another couple, Ed and Susan, felt an immediate attraction to one another and sensed that each had finally found the "right" relationship. Ed had been twice married and divorced and Susan had divorced and considered herself "fiercely independent." Each had children from their previous marriages. According to Ed, he had a "sense of being with the right person for the first time," and Susan felt as if her feelings for Ed were exactly what she had been "looking for forever."

Although their attraction was undeniable, the relationship has not always been perfect. Shortly after their marriage, Susan decided to leave for a month to reconsider their marriage and her life's direction. At the time, Ed decided he would love her and remain thankful they had come together, regardless of whether or not she returned. Later, after they reconciled, Ed would have his own problems with work, unresolved issues from former relationships, and a sense that he was succumbing to a loss of direction (and alcohol). Part of their ongoing challenge has been trying to resolve the fact that "both of us want to be quarterbacks on this two-person team."

And yet, their love for each other has persisted. Psychic readings have put them together repeatedly as a couple and as brother and sister. Regardless of their past-life connections, the patterns they seem to share are those of "carrying for each other, teaching each other, and supporting each other." After years of being together, Ed has found a sense of self-worth by being with Susan, and Susan has found a sense of belonging and letting down some of her previous "defense mechanisms." Ed has gotten over his addictive behaviors and Susan finally feels as though she can settle down. Together, each has helped the other enhance their respective relationships with their children. After ten years, they still look forward to being together.

Even after more than forty years, another couple, Bob and Diane Aaron, still feel "incomplete" when they are apart. From his perspective, Bob always knew that "I would get married to the right woman." However, when he first met Diane he was "not very impressed," even though she was nice, attractive, intelligent, and a good conversationalist. Still, he had no intention of asking her out. Six months later they happened to run into each other again "by chance," and Bob decided to ask her out anyway. Within three months they were engaged and within six months they were married.

Their life together has been full and rewarding. Although communication between the two has not always been easy, there was always "the underlying assurance of unconditional love between us." The parents of four children, child rearing presented the most opportunities for disagreement and conflict, although Bob and Diane "adjusted to each others' needs in parenting and became a unified front." According to Diane, "I expressed many times to our children that my love for my husband came first and I wanted that to be the same for them in their lives with their mates. Throughout our life together we have somehow learned to get the love going more often than the need to be right."

Although uncertain as to specific lifetimes, Diane is convinced that she and Bob "have been together in many lifetimes. We really think alike. The feeling is one of being in sync and comfortable. This is not the first time we have been together, nor will it be the last." In reflecting upon their relationship, she adds, "We worked well together, complemented each other in our abilities, felt a need to be together, and a desire to significantly share and experience spiritual development."

Challenges within the last couple of years have included learning how to accept "lovingly and unconditionally" the surprising news that their son is a homosexual and Bob's recent diagnosis of cancer. Even now, the couple face their challenging experiences with much talk, prayer, unconditional love, and an unwavering commitment to each other.

In terms of their differences, Bob states: "Our differences seem to complement our marriage. Between the two of us we can usually solve or work out any problem or opportunity." Without a doubt, the couple believe their commitment to spirituality "has been a bedrock for our relationship."

Soul mate relationships are not limited to relationships between men and women. Pam and Christine have shared a relationship for more than ten years. Meeting one another at work, Pam recalls first seeing Christine walking up a flight of stairs. There was an instant attraction. Immediately, the thought went through Pam's mind, "There she is!" The two began dating shortly thereafter.

Early on in their relationship, Pam had a dream in which she and Christine were on a playground. All of a sudden, a tidal wave appeared out of nowhere and began heading toward the couple. Before they were hit, each grabbed the hands of the other just as the water swept over them. As the waters receded, the couple found themselves still standing in the same position, facing each other and holding hands. As it turned out, the dream was precognitive. The first weekend the couple went away together on vacation (playground), word reached them that Christine's father had died unexpectedly and suddenly of a heart attack (tidal wave). The vacation quickly ended, and Pam took Christine back to her mother's home. Years later, Pam would add,

"The dream has also symbolized our deep connection, illustrated by the simple act of joining hands and just holding on."

A few months after their first date, Pam and Christine moved in together. They shared a deep connection and an ease of communication. They often stated that they were "meant" to be. In spite of that fact, Pam couldn't help shake the fear that she was going to lose Christine. One night she awoke from a dream and seemed to be in some state of confusion:

> I awoke in the middle of the night, wondering who was lying beside me. An immediate impression came to mind: " . . . it's okay, it's A_____." I felt that the person was male and that "his" name began with an "A." There was an image of a Civil War soldier (North), and I felt as though we had fought together perhaps as brothers. Suddenly I felt angry that "he" had died fifteen years before I had in that experience.

All at once, Pam realized that the person lying next to her was actually Christine. However, that experience helped to explain part of their connection as well as Pam's unfounded concern about losing her.

In addition to the possible Civil War experience, the couple believe they may have been twins in a past life because their connection has felt so strong. However, the same feeling has had the effect of keeping each of them somewhat subdued in their individual expressions because neither wanted to be that much different than the other. In terms of difficulties, Pam and Christine think that their greatest challenges have been the deaths of their fathers and the time Pam was interested in another woman. They've worked through those difficulties because neither was willing to give up what they had found. They have also learned a lot from one another. According to Pam:

I've learned a great deal about patience, persistence, and loyalty from Christine. Whereas I tend to be unsettled and dissatisfied with everyday life, Christine takes it in stride, finding joy in the moment. Whereas I tend to flit from one thing to another, she delves deeply. In terms of what I've taught her, I think it is that there are golden, unplanned moments in life if we just allow them to happen. I've also taught her that giving people the benefit of the doubt allows them, and you, to grow and to change.

For Christine's part, she says:

I have gained a lot in my personal growth, from Pam's sense of adventure and her ability to see situations from a different perspective because of her keen insight and perceptions. Pam likes to experiment with new things—maybe following a new pursuit only for a short time. On the other hand, I tend to stay with something until I'm a "pro" and the activity consumes a great deal of my time. In this respect, I think our energies, together, help us strike a balance as we grow—each learning to be a little more like the other. The greatest gift we have to offer the other is constancy. Whatever challenges arise (even about our relationship) we "stand fast" together and support one another.

In another example from the Cayce archives, John and Peggy Carlson were brought together at college because of their mutual interest in music. John was born in China to Christian missionaries and Peggy grew up in a small town in Michigan. Although the statistical odds of coming together might have seemed astronomical with such beginnings, it happened nonetheless.

While he was still a boy, John's parents returned to the United States and he ended up going to college in Massachusetts as a ministerial student. At one point, he took a break from Massachusetts and decided to go to Northland College in Wisconsin for a year. At about the same time, Peggy was an accomplished pianist and a student at a small junior college. One night the choir director from Northland came to her junior college for a performance and the accompanist didn't show up, so Peggy was invited to play. Afterward, the choir director insisted that he wanted her at Northland. She transferred to Northland and even got a job in the administration office. She recalls the first time she saw John was from a photograph:

> I was working in the office and flipping through the folders of the incoming students. I can remember stopping and looking at the picture of John. As soon as I saw his picture, I just knew I was going to marry him. I just knew it. I didn't love him because I didn't even know him. But somehow, I just knew he was the one.

Finally, they met in person because they had the opportunity to sing together in the choir. In fact, Peggy had to work with John quite a bit, teaching him his part. From that day forward, music would be an important part of their lives together. Shortly thereafter, they were married. Prior to their marriage, John's mother had told Peggy, "If you marry John, you won't have an easy life, but it will never be dull." Her statement had been prophetic.

By this time, John's mother had become a writer and had written a review of the Cayce biography, *There Is a*

*River,* for a Methodist publication. As a result, both John and Peggy became involved in the work of Edgar Cayce and each obtained life readings. The readings confirmed the fact that the two had known each other many times previously.

John possessed an excellent singing and speaking voice. His reading encouraged him to cultivate both and to direct them into spiritual pursuits. According to the reading, in the past he had once used music for sensual purposes and could fall into the same temptation in the present. Cayce told him that the purpose of his present lifetime was to complete the same work he had begun during the time of the early Church in Laodicea. John apparently had been present during much of the turmoil that had threatened to undermine the early Church; yet, through it all, he had somehow managed to maintain his faith. That strength of conviction remained with him in the present.

Prior to his lifetime in Laodicea, John had been an or- derly to Joshua, Moses' scribe. From that period he was well acquainted with the law and possessed a deep re- spect for spirituality. At the same time, however, he had become prone to emphasize the letter of the law rather than its spirit. When frustrated, he was also inclined to emotional outbursts and rash decisions. Cayce advised him to learn to control his temper.

In Egypt, John had been very active in the temples with music and instruments such as the harp and the cymbals. During that lifetime, however, instead of using his music as a service for others, he had used music as a means of arousing bodily sensations and had turned in- stead to the "fleshpots" of Egypt. In terms of his love of music, Cayce warned him, "Let it not tempt thee as in the days of Egypt . . . " (3188-1). In the present, music was to be a hobby that helped him in his spiritual pursuits.

Peggy had also helped hold the early Church together

in Laodicea. At that time, she had used psalm-singing to inspire others. In the present, she was told that in order to keep harmony in her home and hold it together she would need to draw upon those same musical talents. In terms of her relationship with John, she was told, "For you'll have a hard time keeping him in line, in his activities!" (5070-1). At the time of Joshua, Peggy had been one of the sisters of Rahab who helped entertain the spies that were sent into Jericho to destroy the city. Joshua and his men saved her and her family because of her kindness. Afterward, she was accepted into the tribe of Judah and came to know of the wonders of the God, Jehovah. Previously, during a lifetime in ancient Egypt, Peggy was told that she had worked in one of the temples, preparing individuals for motherhood.

Because of some of her past-life activities, Peggy had a very hard time in the present with self-respect and having confidence in herself. Her reading told her to work at not being so self-conscious. One of the main purposes of her life's work was to be "the home," providing an environment for the raising of children. She was to use her love of music in conjunction with the spiritual work of her husband. Several times she was warned that she would have a challenge keeping him in line. She had also used music less than purposefully in the past at a dance hall. For that reason, when she inquired whether or not a certain university was the best place to finish her master's degree, she was told, "If that's a good place to learn how to build a home, do it; if it's a good place to learn how to entertain, forget it."

While still in college, Peggy had an experience that she felt confirmed her lifetime as Rahab's sister. She was watching a movie about the biblical characters Naomi and Ruth. She became so caught up in the story and the emotions it brought up within her that she couldn't get it out of her mind. For the longest time, the story would come to her, and she would begin to cry just thinking about it. It didn't make any sense to her to feel that depth of emotion until finally, in one of her religion classes, she realized that if she had been one of Rahab's sisters, then she had been Ruth's aunt and had actually seen the story firsthand!

Together, John and Peggy had five children. From the very first, their parenting styles were very different. John had been brought up with severe discipline. As a child, he had also been given an overabundance of structure and long lists of things for him to do. As a result, for years John felt the same need to create lists for himself, his wife, and his children. Peggy once told friends, "I got to be so sick of lists!" He was also stern and could sometimes be fierce and quick to anger. Peggy was easygoing and more lax in discipline. Sometimes, when the children were young, she felt the need to protect them from his emotional outbursts. Over the years, John had to learn to mellow, and to some degree Peggy had to learn to become firmer and more structured.

In time, John obtained graduate degrees and became an excellent professor, a writer, a pastoral counselor, and a psychotherapist. He was also an excellent speaker and inspired audiences around the world. In spite of his many talents, just as Cayce had predicted, Peggy often had a hard time keeping him "in line" on several fronts. While living in New York State, John was a teacher at a beautiful university campus. Peggy considered that time in their life together as one of her favorites. She and the children were happy and John was voted the best teacher on campus for several years in a row. As a result of his ability to inspire young people with religious education, the dean wanted to keep John working with the freshman classes. John, however, wanted to work with more serious graduate students. Rather than seeking a compromise, one day John just quit. Peggy was devastated about leaving the university, their home, and their community, but John would not be dissuaded.

Later, when her husband was teaching at another university and Peggy and the children had become settled and happy, a day came when John decided to leave just as abruptly. He had wanted to work on a book for the university; the administration had wanted him to build up the department and its curriculum. Again, there was no effort made at a compromise. Peggy once reported, "I was just in awe of John—if he said it, I figured it was truth. It was gospel. I didn't question him a whole lot."

In terms of their personal relationship, on two occasions John was not feeling very fulfilled in his work. On both occasions, he became interested in another woman. At first, Peggy could do nothing but cry and feel devastated. However, the first time it happened, another man showed his own interest in Peggy and she told her husband, "If you want her, you can have her. I'm going to pursue other relationships myself." John dropped the idea of seeing the other woman that same day. Years later, the second time it happened with another woman, Peggy told her husband, "Our marriage is over—I'm giving you to her." Again, John dropped the idea of the relationship. Peggy once reported that these two incidents helped her have more self-respect and more self-confidence than just about anything else that happened in her life. In spite of his temptation, on his own part, John couldn't imagine living life without Peggy.

As the years passed, John did a great deal of traveling and always wanted Peggy to be with him. Outsiders saw the couple as inseparable. More and more frequently, he took Peggy into his thinking, and he shared things with her. She would later state, "I never got the feeling that he was bored talking or sharing with me."

In the 1970s, John and Peggy cofounded a small nonprofit research and academic center designed to help

churches, ministers, and individuals interested in spirituality and religious education. According to Peggy, she
and John had come to believe that "a husband and wife
ought to do something together in which they can be a
team. There's got to be something beyond children and
living together, some kind of service that a couple can
do together." That togetherness also extended to their
love of music, and throughout their lives together music
played an important role in choirs, churches, and educational programs in which the two participated. In
time, John and Peggy began to feel that their relationship was extremely important, even "a covenant" under
God. And within that covenant each had much to teach
the other. According to Peggy:

> If I could help young couples realize that you
> don't come together by chance. One of the difficult
> things of being a partner is that you often attract
> someone very different from you. At first, you think
> that the person is ignoring you or not caring about
> you because they don't like the same things that you
> like. Learn to honor the differences, appreciate the
> differences. Allow yourself to be taught by the other
> person and remember what a gift it is to have a part-
> ner.

At the end of their lives together, Peggy, reflecting on
more than fifty years of marriage, said, "I've been so very
blessed":

> From John, I learned what it was to get conscious.
> I live in the moment a lot. I take what life hands me
> and give back what I can. The first half of my life I
> lived by default. John taught me how to stay con-
> scious. He helped me to value consciousness. I val-
> ued feelings and religious experiences. I could just

live in the warmth of people and what's happening right now. He helped me to see that you have a great deal of input in creating your life's situations. From me, he tried to learn how to flow. How to trust. How to trust relationships. How to trust that God would meet us in terms of money. He always had that Depression frame-of-mind where you feel like, "I may not be able to eat tomorrow, so I better get filled up today." He felt that secondhand things were the best you could have.

When John lay dying, he looked up at his wife from his bed, reached out to take her hand, and said, "Peggy, I'm not afraid of death, but I don't want to leave you. I don't want to lose you."

Peggy simply smiled back at him and said, "Look, you were born in China and I was born in the boondocks of Michigan. Somehow, we found each other—don't worry, we'll find each other again."

# 3

## *Soul Mates as Family*

Any human life situation is like the momentary position
of a kaleidoscope; and the group of souls within that
situation are like the bits of brightly colored glass which
form an interesting pattern of relationship. Then the kaleidoscope is shaken . . . and with this flick of the wrist
there comes into being a new design, a new combination of elements. And so on again and again, time after
time, always different . . . always it is significant, and always there is a dynamic and purposeful intention . . .

Gina Cerminara, Ph.D.
*Many Lives, Many Loves*

In 1930 parents of a seventeen-year-old girl brought
their daughter, Wendy, to the Cayce hospital because
of a painful physical condition (275-1). Doctors had di-
agnosed the problem as an erosion of the head of the
femur of one of her legs—cancer of the hip—and stated
that the condition was incurable. By following the advice in the readings, Wendy was eventually cured of her

cancer and lived to be eighty years old. What is interesting about this case in terms of soul mate relationships,
however, is that eight members of Wendy's immediate
family eventually received readings describing how the
family had been brought together in various relationship
situations for thousands of years. Apparently, members
of the family had been associated in a series of lifetimes
that included ancient Egypt, Persia, Greece, Rome, Germany, and early America. Literally hundreds of pages of
readings and documentation detail the lives of these individuals and the past-life connections among them as
well as with various members of their extended families.

While discussing their soul mate connection, Cayce
stated that most of the present family had been together
in Rome. During that period, certain family members
had been followers of the early Christian sect—some following the work begun by the apostle Peter, others more
interested in the philosophy of Paul. A few individuals
had also been responsible for some small measure of
persecution against the Christians. The entire experience had created an interesting influence on the present
family dynamic. The father [378], Franz, was told in one
of his readings that during the Roman period, "the entity
became associated with many of those that are in the
entity's own household in the present, and their contacts, their aids, their fallings away, are necessary for the
developments of all so associated in the present" (378-
12).

It was because of her Roman lifetime that Wendy was
now experiencing bone cancer. Apparently, during the
time of Nero, she had enjoyed watching the physical
combat and persecution of the Christians in the arena.
In order to experience firsthand the physical suffering
and pain of a situation she had once made fun of, at a
soul level Wendy had chosen the hip condition. When
she asked why she had waited nearly 2,000 years to meet

this condition, Cayce told her that it was because she "couldn't do it before!" (275-25). The necessary elements to bring the situation together had only occurred in her present lifetime.

In addition to the Roman influence, the family had many other experiences and situations from the past that were having an effect upon their feelings, talents, and opinions in the present. A brief synopsis of some of those past-life connections is as follows:

In ancient Egypt, Wendy and her present sister Kate, [276], had come to know each other in one of the temples. Kate had arrived from another country to learn about the wonders of Egypt; Wendy was an instructor in the temple. The two had become close friends. At that time, both women possessed musical talents and had aided others to attune to the highest within themselves through music. In this life, Cayce told Wendy and Kate that each still possessed the gift of music; he suggested the girls work with the harp and the flute, respectively. As the years passed, Cayce's insight proved to be correct. Both girls became well-known performing artists and were still performing in the 1970s.

During the Egyptian period as well, Wendy's mother, Lorraine, [255], had found herself in a "combative" relationship with a male associate. Although the two worked together, they were often at odds in terms of their differing ideas. To enable both souls to work through the experience, in the present the male co-worker had reincarnated as Lorraine's son Ben, [452], a Lutheran minister with very different philosophical ideas than his mother's. Lorraine wanted to give a life reading to her son, but Ben found the idea appalling and refused to consider the possibility of reincarnation. He was not interested in his mother's beliefs or philosophy. Eventually, Lorraine asked how she could best deal with her son and was told, "in *loving* tolerance, in loving association, ever being ready to answer when any aid or help must be given or may be given" (255-12).

Finally, because Ben suffered from allergies and hay fever, Lorraine insisted that she obtain a physical reading for him. Reluctantly, because nothing else had been able to help him, Ben agreed. After the reading was obtained, he followed the suggestions. To his surprise, he felt so much better that he decided to open to the other information in the Cayce readings, and he eventually asked for his own life reading. It wasn't long before Ben became as excited about his mother's philosophy as she was, and the two reconciled their differing viewpoints. Lorraine wrote that the whole thing "makes me feel very happy. Patience has been rewarded. It took just two years to convince him . . . "

The readings indicated that Franz and Lorraine had been married previously. Although he was head of the family in the present, he had also helped nearly every member of the family in ancient Egypt. In this life he was a very successful and wealthy businessman. For his own learning, however, he needed to meet a situation that he had apparently created during a lifetime in Germany. At that time, he had spiritually regressed because of his own doubts, fears, and disillusionment. Apparently, he had reached a point in that life when he had simply given up. Those same past-life feelings and fears had to repeat themselves and be overcome in the present.

In spite of his financial success, Franz lost millions of dollars and nearly everything he owned during the Depression. As a result, he gave up all hope and even contemplated suicide. Not knowing what else to do, for five months Franz disappeared from his family and friends and simply wandered throughout the country. No one knew where he was or what he was doing. During that time, the very people he had helped in the past now had to help him with their prayers, their hope, and their on-

going love. It was only after much introspection on his
own part and many prayers and concerns on his family's
part that Franz eventually returned home. After his arrival in September 1934, he wrote Edgar Cayce:

> Some five months ago my affairs seemed so
> hopeless, the tangle so muddled, that I could not
> see my way out. Now, thanks to [much reading] . . .
> and the deep understanding and love of my good
> wife, everything is changing completely. It is a real
> miracle to watch how God is unfolding for us a glo-
> rious and wonderful plan for a happy new career,
> and all through scientific prayer. Almost each day
> some new development is bringing us nearer to our
> ultimate goal of establishing a happy home, where I
> can be actively engaged in business, applying the
> principles that I have absorbed by being guided
> into the path of right thoughts . . . Had I known what
> I know today, everything would be different. I had
> been living in Fool's Paradise and needed this shock
> to cleanse my soul . . . Case 378-50 Report File

Franz had apparently overcome his fears from the past
and even grown in the process. The same had been true
of Wendy's situation with the bone cancer and Lorraine
and Ben's antagonistic feelings toward one another.
Other family members experienced their own challenging relationships and situations—all of which provided
them, ultimately, with the lessons in soul growth that
needed to be learned. Just as Cayce had suggested, the
entire family had been drawn together for a purposeful
experience. By being with one another, each had been
provided with the opportunity to evolve, to grow, and to
become a better person in the process.

According to the Edgar Cayce readings, between
earthly incarnations a soul takes stock of all it has come

to know as well as all it needs to learn in this ongoing process of personal growth and development. Once this evaluation process is complete and the individual has decided what lessons might possibly be achieved next on the soul's learning agenda, the soul waits for the proper timing and location that will best provide the opportunities the soul needs to experience. A soul chooses individuals with whom it has been associated before and suddenly the present-day family grouping is created. Personal wholeness is achieved as each soul completes each lesson in soul growth and personal transformation.

When a sixteen-year-old girl asked, "For what purpose did I choose my present parents in this incarnation?" she was told: "For thine own enlightenment, and thy parents' understanding" (2632-1). In another instance, Cayce told a fourteen-year-old girl that she had previously been associated with her parents on a number of occasions:

> Then, it is not by chance that the entity chose to come into the environ or home into which it came in this experience; but those activities, those associations which have been, make for an awareness, a consciousness that what is needed in the experience may be found there.
>
> Thus, there is brought to the entity an obligation, and to those about the entity a duty—a keeping of that necessary to assist in fulfilling that purpose. 2571-1

When she asked, "For what purpose did I come to my present parents?" she was told, "That ye might gain from their experience and ye be a helpmeet to them in their problems."

When a fifteen-year-old boy asked why he had chosen

to come into the earth at this time and why he had picked his particular family, his reading stated that his family would provide the environment he needed in order to better find himself. In the present, his father was a sea captain and his mother was extremely nurturing and loving. Somehow that environment would prepare him to eventually be of service to others through his innate talent of leadership:

The entity may be an aid to them, as they may be an aid to the entity; a complement one to another.

At this time the entering was for the purpose of giving that which the entity has that many need; the opportunity for self-expression, the opportunity to lend aid to others is before the entity. 984-1

Later reports indicate that [984] was a natural-born leader. He eventually took officer's training in the army and became a captain. After leaving the military, he served in other leadership roles including that of port engineer for the Maryland Port Authority.

When asking about her twin, a thirty-three-year-old artist was told that she and her sister had developed quite a connection to one another at a soul level. So close, in fact, that they had shared a "very close association" with one another in practically every experience in the earth (1789-7). An artist by training, she was told that innately she was a very sensitive and emotional individual. In her most recent life, she had been a spiritualist who had experienced water ducking because of her beliefs. From that episode she had a temper and a tendency to want to "get even" with those who offended her. During a lifetime in France, she had been a student of the work of Rubens—a period from which she had learned her talent for painting. In Persia she had been a sculptress who had developed a keen interest in matters of spirituality. During a lifetime in ancient Egypt she was a decorator of temples and palaces. Throughout each of these experiences, her twin sister had been associated with her in various relationships. Soul mate connections manifest in all manner of relationships over time. Although the relationships we experience with our countless soul mates change, our connection to those individuals (oftentimes both positive and negative) does not.

A sixty-four-year-old woman asked about the connection she had with her father to whom she felt very close. Cayce told her that in Persia he had been her uncle, although he had raised her. In the Holy Land, he had been the father of some of her friends, but she had eventually come to live with the family. And, in a lifetime just previous to the present during the early settling of Georgia, he had been a very close associate (3356-1).

In 1941, an eleven-year-old girl was told that she had once been a spy in Palestine in which she had often found it necessary to "check up" on the exploits of her present-day father. In this life, although close friends, the two found it necessary to often question the activities of each other because of that earlier association (2572-1).

From Cayce's perspective, family relationships are drawn together based upon past associations that have been positive and negative. In the present, however, the situation occurs in order to give every member of the family an opportunity to become a little more whole at the level of the soul. As is evidenced in a number of Cayce readings, when a couple is expecting a child, various souls might consider the prospect of having such a couple as parents as well as the probable experiences that couple will provide. Regardless of how wonderful or how harsh such a family environment might appear to the outside world, the choice to come into that family is made at a soul level only if the situation has the potential to provide the soul with the curriculum it needs. In other words, the readings make it clear that we choose our parents.[4]

The idea that a soul would purposefully choose a harmful or an abusive family relationship may be impossible for some people to comprehend. However, the soul is most concerned with the possibilities of what might come out of the situation rather than with the specifics of the situation itself. For example, a soul with a great deal of empathy and the innate talents of a counselor might choose to be born to an abusive parent in order to experience (and work through) that situation. Afterward, as an adult, that soul would be well equipped to help others deal with the very same situation. At a soul level, we choose life situations that will best enable us to learn and to fulfill the purposes for which we came into the earth at this time. Whether or not those lessons are learned, however, remains a matter of free will.

As an example from the Cayce archives, in 1942 a thirty-seven-year-old woman, Matty, obtained a life reading. Although she had many soul qualities, in one of her previous experiences Matty had purposefully taken advantage of another person, Angela, almost destroying that individual's life in the process. At that same time, Angela had apparently acquired a great deal of anger and resentment toward the woman—not seeing, perhaps, that her own difficult experience had been an opportunity to be a helpful lesson. In order for both women to work through the situation in this life, Angela had decided to be born blind and mentally disabled to Matty, the same woman who had taken advantage of her previously. As a mother, Matty now had to learn how to be of loving service to a soul she had once harmed. When

---

[4]This process of choosing one's family environment is covered in greater detail in the chapter "Conception and Soul Attraction."

asked about the difficulty of working through the experience, Cayce told Matty: "Do not feel sorry for self, but rather give glory to God for giving thee the opportunity to meet thyself and to see His love, His forgiveness, manifested in the earth" (2796-1). Many relationship examples in the Cayce files make it clear that soul mate relationships often entail some measure of anger, animosity, and resentment that both individuals are required to work through.

A thirty-six-year-old woman received a physical reading for a condition that included neurosis. The reading stated that some of her problems were due to her own selfish nature and the animosity and hate she held toward members of her family. Although a life reading was never procured to discover the source of the antagonism, it became clear that she and her family were definitely at odds. Cayce advised her to begin to eliminate all of the anger from her life, "For, remember, unless we may learn to love that something in even those who have been and are our enemies, we have not begun to think straight." As if oblivious to his suggestion, she later wrote about the bitterness she still felt:

> As to life: I'm very disgusted due that I'm not a young girl and being the oldest of the family, it seems that I was just downed so much and as a young girl never allowed to do anything. I was always reminded that I'm the oldest and setting a bad example. Now it seems my family got me so under their feet, that at times I'm sick of living. It seems there is nothing to live for. I'm too attached to my family. I think the world of them, and I try so hard but it seems I just have no luck of winning them over. I'm the one [who] always has to take the worst of everything; whether it's in company or just family it seems I'm always cut short, always in the

wrong. I work for the past twenty years in the same
factory and find no trouble with my co-workers.
And yet home I have it so hard. Case 3254-1 Report
File

On another occasion, a thirty-four-year-old housewife wanted to know why she was born into a family with
which "I've never had anything in common." Cayce replied, "Ye had nothing in common with them as ye applied thyself in the experience before this. As the tree
falls, so will it lie. So is the law given." When she asked
about why she had experienced such an unhappy childhood, she was told, "Happiness is a state of consciousness. It is found within self. Ye had not found thyself, nor
thy relationship to the Creative Forces as may manifest
in this material world" (2982-1).

A twenty-eight-year-old woman asked Edgar Cayce
about the advisability of trying to gain custody of her
young daughter who was living with her ex-husband.
The woman had remarried and wondered whether or
not it would be best for the child to live with her. Cayce
told her that the situation had come to pass because in
her most recent lifetime she and her daughter had been
sisters, although the two had never gotten along. The
present experience was in order to enable her to make a
conscious decision to have a relationship with her
daughter, a situation about which Cayce replied, "You
can . . . Will you?" (3573-1).

From the Cayce files, it becomes apparent that soul
mate relationships with family members are an ongoing
learning process. Sometimes those relationships have
been very positive and sometimes those experiences
have been negative. It is also common for past-life influences among individuals to contain elements of both.
For example, a father, [2385], found that he felt both love
and jealousy toward his young son, [1990]. As the boy

grew, the rivalry between the two increased so that often their relationship was one of animosity. Past-life connections included lifetimes when they had been close companions, as well as an incarnation when the two had repeated the father-son relationship. It was a lifetime in early America, however, that had apparently created the present-day rivalry. During that period, the boy had been very close to his sister—who in the present was his mother. At the time, his sister had married someone the boy found disreputable and unworthy—his current father. Interestingly enough, the father's present-day job eventually took the family to the very city in which the past-life rivalry had occurred. According to the reports on file, the situation between father and son was eventually healed.

In a contemporary example, Gail felt very close to her son, Larry, when he was a baby. During his birth, she watched him being born through the reflection in the birthing room's mirror. Like many mothers, she felt that "It was the most exciting, fulfilling event of my life up to that point." However, by the time Larry was around the age of five or six, her feelings toward the boy were more mixed: "I found myself not only not liking him some of the time, but really hating him." This sense of animosity lasted for years, causing Gail to feel awful. In order to help heal the situation, she began working with prayer and asking for forgiveness. Finally, the memories of two past lives came to her in dreams. Because of those experiences, she was able to understand what her "hate" was all about and to release it.

According to Gail, Larry had a habit that would make the "hairs rise on my neck." During mealtimes he would often look at his mother, snap his fingers, and say, "Get me so-and-so." Although the act made her extremely angry, Gail found herself getting up and retrieving exactly what her son had requested. This went on for a number of years until Larry was eighteen. At that time, Gail had a dream in which she saw her son as a desert nomad, carrying her off as a captive to his city. In the dream, she was added to the nomad's harem and became his "favorite." Although a captive, at that time Gail grew to love the man but she "always resented having to come when called." Because Gail and her son had discussed the topic of reincarnation previously, after having the dream she explained what she had seen to Larry. From that day forward, he dropped his habit of snapping his fingers to summon her and it was never repeated.

Another past-life influence seemed to come to her whenever she was working in the kitchen, preparing dinner, and Larry would be hanging around causing some kind of friction. While Gail was using a butcher knife, her son would make her so intensely angry that she would find herself saying, "I'd just like to take this knife and scalp you!" Later she had a dream in which she saw her son scalp her on a field of battle in Mongolia. Once she understood where her feelings of anger originated, she could let them go.

In addition to the lifetimes where these negative patterns of behavior originated, Gail is convinced that she and Larry have also been together previously in a number of very positive experiences, including Egypt and a lifetime as American Indians. While she was taking a trip to Egypt, Gail repeatedly had an overwhelming emotional experience in which she desperately wanted her son to be with her. Especially at some of the temples, Gail's "longing" for her son was "a gut reaction so strong that it would almost double me over."

As to the Indian lifetime, Gail loved to ride horses while she was growing up and even owned her own horses in high school. One of her favorite things was to ride bareback. After she married and had children, neither she nor her children had the opportunity to ride.

However, when Larry was older, she took him to a ranch that had horses. While there, Larry got himself a rope and went after some of the "wild horses" that were on the property. Some time later, everyone was surprised to find him riding one of the horses with no bridle, saddle, or bit, just a rope around the creature's neck. He seemed to know just how to guide the horse only with pressure from his thighs and calves—an old Indian skill.

Over time, Gail has learned to trust her feelings and to talk openly with her son about everything. Today there is unconditional love and understanding between them. Gail says that "The older we have gotten, the more considerate we have become of each other, the more supportive we have become in all situations, and the more we have come to appreciate each other with deep and abiding love." Even though they live more than a thousand miles apart, they still possess a strong bond of communication between them. Larry seems to know when to call her, just as she knows when to call him.

Rather than thinking that only birth children choose their parents, the Edgar Cayce readings make it clear that adopted children take part in the same selection process. Regardless of where or to whom an individual is born physically, apparently at a soul level the individual has the ability to orchestrate where he or she will end up, thereby having the opportunity to learn whatever lessons are needed.

The adoptive parents of a tenth-month-old boy were told that one of the most influential lifetimes from their son's past was one in which he had been an interpreter of the law in Egypt. In that period he had been associated with and close to both parents. The three had also been together in Persia. From the Egyptian lifetime, the boy, [3346], had also been friends with an individual who in the present was his older brother, adopted into the same family. The reading stated that the two boys had purposefully chosen to be brothers in this life in order to learn from each other's strengths and become better individuals in the process.

A forty-nine-year-old woman was told that she had also taken care of her adopted child during a lifetime in Palestine. The boy had come to her because of that experience and together they could create a "closeness of purpose" in the present (2787-1). In another example, parents of an adopted three-year-old boy were told that their son had known his "physical parents" would give him up at birth. The adoptive couple had attracted their son into their family in the present because of the environment they could provide for him as well as because of their mutual interests; the three had also been together previously (3340-1).

In 1944, family members asked about the advisability of telling their grown daughter that she had been adopted. Cayce replied that they could do so as long as it was in a manner that clearly defined the deep sense of connection that soul still had with the family. He reminded them that birth parents had a choice of their offspring only at a soul level, whereas adoptive parents had that same choice as well as a choice at a physical level. In the language of the readings, "a mother, a father, may not choose one that may be born to them, except spiritually. In adoption, the choice may be spiritual and material" (3673-1).

A twenty-nine-year-old man wanted to know why he had been separated from his parents at such an early age. He was told that it had been a choice made at a soul level in order to give him the very situation he needed in this particular experience (2301-1).

In another example from the present, two women, Dotty and Carol, have had a relationship "as sisters" for half a century. In actuality the two are cousins, who came together because both of Dotty's parents had died by the time she was eight. Dotty came to live with her aunt's family (her mother's sister). At the time, her aunt had her own little girl, Carol, who was four. According to Carol, "We are cousins but consider ourselves sisters, as does the rest of our family . . . We have shared thoughts, dreams, fears, clothes, and laughter for more than fifty years."

At first, coming to live with her aunt's family was, in some ways, as traumatic an experience for Dotty as losing both of her parents. She had to leave her friends and remaining family behind in Virginia and move to her aunt's and uncle's house in Florida. As might be expected, Dotty was apprehensive and fearful; on the other hand, Carol was excited: "I was happy to have a sister, someone to share my room." Despite their age differences and their differing looks, personalities, likes and dislikes, the two girls became fast friends and really enjoyed being with each other. In a very short time, it felt as though Dotty had always been a member of the family and she felt she belonged. Although Carol had a brother, it was Dotty to whom she was always closest.

Growing up, disagreements between the two were few and far between. It was a bond that seemed unexplainable. As teenagers, they defended one another to friends, to other family members, and to their parents even when it might have been easier not to do so. As a result, very often both girls ended up on restrictions for what one did and not the other. They used to play tricks on each other and laugh for having done so. Carol remembers, "I could lie out my clothes for school and go in the bathroom, came back to our room and since she caught an earlier bus, she would have left for school wearing what I had laid out for myself."

In terms of a past-life connection, Carol has frequently had dreams in which she and Dotty appear to be living in the Dominican Republic in a pastel house on a hill overlooking the pale green water. In the present, the two are convinced they shared a past life in the tropics. Although white in the present, both believe they have recently had incarnations with beautiful dark skin. Even now, they "share a love of Calypso music, Harry Belafonte, and tropical foods." Dotty loves wild, bright colors and gems. Both women are drawn to the stories told by Jamaicans and Dominicans of their acquaintance about their lives "back home."

In this life, a major family tragedy occurred with the death of Carol's father. At the age of forty-nine, he committed suicide. According to Carol:

> My father's death was traumatic for both of us. We were very close to him. He was the one who took us to all our activities, listened to us relate how our dates went, waited for us to get home before going to bed. He truly listened to us. Even though he was a strict disciplinarian, he was always there for us, if for nothing else than talking . . . we still think about how much we miss him.

His death put both girls in a state of shock, which they were able to work through together: talking, sharing feelings, and discussing all the things that each wished they had said or done. Although they are separated by geography, even now the two often handle challenges in the same way—"together."

Their mutual understanding and connection to each other have helped both women get through many of life's roughest periods. According to the women, often we just "KNOW we need to call each other. We have often said that we have a major investment in 'Ma Bell,' especially during some critical times." Ironically, although Dotty moved from Virginia to live with Carol's family in Florida, today and for the last forty years Carol has lived in Virginia and Dotty has remained in Florida.

As to what each has taught the other, they have learned about compassion and a friendship that is unconditional. In spite of their busy lives, they always have time for each other, time to listen, time to share, time to simply be there for the other person. Carol says:

> Our relationship sustains us. Many miles separate us now, but we talk at least once a week (usually twice). We are always there for each other. Dotty makes little lists to remind her about the things she wants to be sure and tell me. The greatest issue we have in our lives right now is when and where we will be able to retire so that we can be in closer proximity to each other . . .
>
> Our relationship has grown over the years but in a lot of ways it has stayed the same. There was a period in our lives when we both were busy with small children and didn't communicate as often as we do now, but the feeling has always been there. No relationship that either of us have had has the same sense of closeness and knowing each other so well. It is truly as if we have known each other forever.

# 4

## Soul Mates as Friends

There is nothing by chance. Friendships are only the *renewing* of former purposes, ideals. For, as the preacher gave, "There is nothing new under the sun" . . . Isn't the last apple also that portion of the first one created?

Edgar Cayce reading 2946-2

"She was my best friend," Tina says about her childhood friend, Lauren. "She was the first person I felt comfortable around. I was very shy, she was more outgoing." The two were in the sixth grade and lived about a half-mile apart. Although they had seen each other in school, neither realized that they lived in the same neighborhood until the final weeks of sixth grade. Each was out walking the family dog; Tina had a collie and Lauren was with a schnauzer. According to Tina, "We saw each other walking our dogs and I remember we started commenting on each other's pet. We both loved animals. From that day forward, we made a decision to be best friends."

All through that summer, Tina and Lauren began to

"hang out." They kept journals together, writing beside each other. They read together. They listened to music. They played games and drew pictures together. They spent every weekend together, taking turns between the two households—each becoming a member of the other's family: "We used to go to each other's church on Sundays, but when I went to her Presbyterian Church, I still had to go to mine (Catholic). I thought that was strange because when she went to mine that was enough for her. At the time I wondered, 'Why couldn't I go to her church and have it count?'"

All summer long, Lauren and Tina were inseparable. When fall, along with the seventh grade, came, their friendship continued, although both were greatly disappointed that they didn't have any classes together. However, they had frequent opportunities to study together, and, according to Tina, "She was better than I at everything except for math." They wrote notes back and forth and also had the opportunity to work in the school bookstore together, which was considered a real privilege.

They created poems together and wrote out promises to each other in their journals: "I promise to ask that cute boy in church his name and where he goes to school." There weren't really relationships with boys at that point; there were crushes that didn't really go anywhere. They made frequent trips to the neighborhood woods and river, where they would sit on an enormous tree trunk that leaned out over the water; "We'd sit there for hours and just talk." They were forever redecorating their bedrooms to make them look more like Mary Tyler Moore's apartment. Both were in Girl Scouts, so they went camping together. Tina recalls:

> She was one of the first people I ever met who befriended me and liked me for who I was. I never felt that I had an ally until I met Lauren. She de-

fended me if someone made fun of me or called me "chubby." I always accepted her and loved her. We just loved being in each other's company, no matter what we were doing. For hours, we used to lie down on our backs and watch the clouds float by—seeing what shapes we could see dancing overhead. We didn't know it at the time, but we were both very deep and spiritual and had conversations that would have probably surprised those around us. It was one of those safe friendships when it was okay to tell the person, "You're my best friend."

The friendship was the stabilizing force in their lives for two-and-a-half years, until Lauren's father was transferred to the West Coast. As the eighth grade came to a close and both knew that Lauren would be moving, the two made an agreement that "we would never say goodbye." Instead, they would simply say, "See ya." When Lauren left, Tina recalls that on the outside she was saying, "See ya," but on the inside she was on the verge of sobbing. Her journal for that day, May 30, 1975, simply says four words: "Lauren left, I cried." Even now, Tina recalls, "It was horribly painful to see her leave; it was just awful. In every sense, it was like a death." At the end of that school year, Lauren had written out some of her own feelings in Tina's yearbook:

I'm really sorry to be leaving you. We've had so many good times these past 2½ years . . . Do you realize how many miles I have walked, walking to and from your house, through the woods, along the beach, up a tree (and back down again) . . . Did you ever realize how many times we acted nuts? How many times we haven't been embarrassed when we should have been? I really don't think I will ever say "goodbye" . . . I can just see our letters to one another now. I'll probably have to send mine in a big fat, Fat, HUGE, manila envelope because it won't fit in a regular one. Too bad we can't just run the ½ mile to each other's houses! Oh well, we'll still be best pals forever . . .

As she had promised, Lauren wrote all the time after that. By her own admission, Tina was never as good at writing letters. The two promised to visit each other, and both families made it possible for Tina to visit Lauren at the end of the ninth grade. Lauren came back to see Tina at the end of the eleventh grade. In 1981, when Lauren got married, Tina flew to California to be her maid of honor. When Tina got married in 1986, Lauren returned to the East to be the matron of honor. The two remained friends by phone and by letter for the next ten years, until Lauren died.

"I wish she hadn't died; it makes it so much harder to think about her now," Tina sighs. "I felt totally safe around her. All through our relationship, it seemed as if I were the younger one and she were older. Whether it was getting married or becoming involved in the arts, she was always ahead of me. She was the leader and I eagerly followed. No matter what else was going on in our lives, the bond of our love remained the same."

After her friend's death, Tina had confirmation about the soul mate connection between them during a hypnotic regression. She saw a lifetime in Scotland when she was Lauren's younger sister:

At that time, she was still the leader. She was older and I was younger. I saw myself sitting there next to her all dressed up in buttons and lace, and I was admiring the buttons and the material I was wearing. I think I spent a lot of time being near her or simply tagging behind. Wherever she was, that's where I wanted to be. Our life was filled with chores, but it was a simple life. As time went on, each of us had similar life experiences: getting married, having children, always going through life's experiences together.

Later, a psychic confirmed the Scottish past life she had seen with Lauren and stated that the two had been together for the course of that entire lifetime. In addition, the psychic told Tina that her friendship with Lauren had been built over a period of 8,000 years and a variety of relationships. Throughout that period, they had learned at a soul level that love transcends time. To be sure, they hadn't always been together—each had soul experiences and lifetimes separate from the other—but in eight incarnations the two had been very closely connected. Examples included Italy when they had been friends in the performing arts and in Egypt where they had come together as co-workers in one of the temples.

Another lifetime was in Geneva, when they were siblings and close friends and had spent a great deal of time writing journals with one another. Their father at the time had also been Tina's father in the present. Throughout the Geneva experience, they were constant companions. They told stories, wrote poetry, and loved to dwell in their imaginations. They possessed similar talents, aspirations, and skills. It was a time when life wasn't so complicated. Life was more clear, simpler, and easier.

All of it made sense to Tina and helped to explain the bond she feels with Lauren, even now:

From Lauren, I got to learn love, and no matter where we went or what happened to us, the love never changed. Until she died, we knew each other longer than any other person. The minute I learned she was dead, I didn't feel any less close to her.

When she moved, I didn't feel any less close to her. It was almost as if the bond between us was eternal, no matter what else was going on in our lives. What I've learned from Lauren is that the bond of love goes though time.

From the perspective of the Edgar Cayce readings, the force that motivates each soul through time and space is the essence of love. In the expression of true love, Cayce believed that the glory of the Creator was somehow manifested in the earth because "God is love!" (1579-1). In friendships, that love somehow inspires each individual to assist the other through life's events. Part of the soul's heritage as a spiritual being is to experience its connection to the Creator through its relationships with other individuals. Cayce believed it was possible for all souls to eventually realize their true relationship with one another and the joint connection they possessed with God. In 1936, a fifty-year-old writer was told:

Hence the necessity of cultivating in the experience of the entity in the present not only earthly friendships, earthly love, but rather that which is the basis *of* or the influence *promoting* same in those relationships as one to another. In other words, that the experience of love is not for the expressions that *self* may be exalted, or that the ones upon whom such is bestowed may be exalted, but rather that the *glory* of the Creative Forces—that prompt same—may be exalted in the earth. 1096-1

In another reading, a very religious sixty-one-year-old woman wanted to know where her deep connection with a dear friend had begun. According to the woman, the two of them had shared "religious ideals" for many years. A reading was given which stated that the two had helped minister to the early Christian sect during the time of the persecutions. That strength of religious conviction remained with both of them in the present, along with the faith that throughout life each would be provided with whatever help was needed to carry on (5025-1).

When a twenty-three-year-old man wanted to know with which individuals he had formed the closest relationships in past lives, Cayce simply replied, "Those who are active in thy associations in the present" (3545-1). A thirty-five-year-old housewife wanted to understand where the closeness she felt between herself and her best friend had originated. Cayce told her that in her most recent lifetime, her present friend had been her daughter (808-18).

A young woman who often experienced problems in her friendships was told that she was frequently misunderstood, causing her friendships to be strained or broken. She was advised to always attempt to rectify those situations, for no individual could have too many friends. He added, "For, love—as friendship—grows by being showered upon others . . . " (951-4).

A teacher wanted to know what had caused the breakup and alienation between herself and another woman who had once been her friend. Edgar Cayce told her that the two had repeated the same pattern of estrangement they had once experienced hundreds of years earlier in France. His advice was to undo what had once been neglected, for "No individual entity has so many friends that it can afford ever to lose a single one" (3234-1).

When a thirty-eight-year-old government clerk wanted to know how he could improve the rough spots in one of his friendships, he was told:

Where there is agreement, these may be made

more secure. Where there is disagreement, do not attempt to convince one another of the veracity of the other as concerning such. This *manner* of approach will weld friendship. When one becomes dependent upon another for *any* form of activity it soon loses its vitality, its virility.

Thus are friendships builded. 622-7

A thirty-nine-year-old woman wanted to know about the past relationship with a male friend of hers from work with whom she was "closely attracted in the present." The reading stated that in her most recent lifetime she had been in New York during its early settling. Apparently, at that time, she had quite an ability to attract members of the opposite sex, always keeping a number of them "on a string"—a trait she could still misuse in the present. During that incarnation, her present friend had been one of her lovers (1935-2).

A beauty salon manager named Sharon was told that she and her friend, Lottie, had been associated in a number of different lifetimes, some as misunderstood rivals and some as very close associates. Those two extremes were best exemplified in lifetimes they had shared in colonial Connecticut and Palestine, respectively. In Connecticut, they had misunderstood one another. At the time, Sharon had been very involved in pursuing freedom of thought and freedom of expression—concepts that were perhaps foreign to Lottie at the time. However, in the Holy Land, the two had often ministered to the needs of those less fortunate than themselves. It was a desire to be of service that remained with both of them in the present (1825-1).

In 1924, a nineteen-year-old girl asked who she knew in the present that had been closely associated with her during a previous lifetime in France. Cayce's response included two of her girlfriends, one from work and another from the neighborhood in which she lived. During the French life, her present neighbor had been her sister and the person to whom she had been closest, and her friend from work had been a nun—a woman she be-friended and often looked to for counsel after entering into the convent herself (288-5).

In a reading given in 1943, a New York dentist discovered that two of his best male friends were individuals with whom he had been closely associated in the past as a trapper. One of them had been his partner and the other had been employed by one of the trading posts to which the two frequently took their pelts. He also discovered that he had known his secretary and his hygienist at the same time. The reading suggested that both women had frequently disagreed with him in the past and had gotten on his nerves—just as they did in the present. On the whole, however, the friendship between them and their ongoing connection with one another were described as "a real asset" to the office (2772-5). From the Cayce files it becomes clear that all of our important relationships in the present had their foundation in the past. As far as the soul is concerned, apparently we do not meet anyone of importance for the very first time.

In a contemporary example of past-life connections between friends, a middle-aged man named Pat was in the travel business and found frequent occasion to journey to Egypt. Over the years, he had made a fast friendship with Mohammed, a native Egyptian. Close in age, each man had his own life, family, and friends, but the friendship they maintained was immediately "picked up again" with each meeting. Mohammed once told his wife, "I don't know why I am always so sorry to see Pat leave." For some reason, Mohammed also felt motivated to take care of his friend and buy him gifts.

During one visit, Mohammed was walking with Pat

through an Egyptian bazaar and the two were discussing the surroundings. For a moment, Pat was distracted by a display in one of the market windows, showcasing Egypt at the beginning of the twentieth century. He stepped aside and looked at the faded pictures of early Egypt. Suddenly, from somewhere inside himself, he had the overwhelming urge to point something out to Mohammed. Without even thinking, he turned around and yelled out, "Hey, Dad, come and look at this!" After that experience, the two were convinced that they had once been father and son.

In another example, two businessmen worked for an international company in their respective countries: one lived in Japan, the other in the United States. When they met, there was an immediate bond of friendship as if they had known each other all their lives. After that, each called the other "my Japanese brother" and "my American brother," respectively. Because of their jobs, they had occasion to travel to each other's country, always looking forward to renewing their friendship.

One day, because the bond between them was so evident, the Japanese man asked a psychic where he had known his "American brother." The psychic replied that the two had been brothers and "carpet salesmen" in the Middle East. What amazed the two men was that shortly thereafter the two were scheduled on a business trip from their respective countries at exactly the same time. The location they were sent was the Middle East.

Another woman recalls the beginning of a thirty-year friendship: "The first time I heard her speak, my soul resonated with the sound of her voice and I felt something shift inside of me." The two, Bonnie and Jean, met during a presentation for a parapsychology course that Bonnie was taking. The professor had introduced the class to his guest speaker for the day, Jean, who would be teaching in his place. At first, Bonnie was frustrated because she had signed up for the course based upon the professor's background and reputation. "I wasn't happy with this new aspect of the class," she recalls. However, as soon as Jean began to speak, Bonnie's disappointment was laid to rest. "I knew I wanted to learn everything she could teach me but more than that, I wanted to learn everything about her."

The longer Jean spoke, the more Bonnie was convinced that there was some kind of a connection between the two of them. In her imagination, she suddenly saw herself in front of the class as well, teaching with Jean. At the time, Bonnie was a wife and mother and had no previous experience as a teacher, but there was definitely a sense of excitement about the prospect.

After class, the two spoke and it became clear that they had a number of things in common. In addition to their interest in the subject matter, they were both drawn to the same types of books, some of the same periods in history, and each was in the midst of family challenges and changes. Recently divorced, Jean was trying to support her three children on her own. For her part, Bonnie had four children, a challenging relationship with her husband, back problems, and a strong sense that something was truly missing from her life. By the time their initial meeting was over, Bonnie felt a strong need to establish a permanent friendship with a woman she had just met: "I have never before or since felt such a strong need to acquire a friendship. It was as though I had no choice."

When the lecture was over, Bonnie found out that Jean was teaching another course so she signed up immediately. As time passed, Bonnie attended all of the classes and made an effort to befriend her teacher. Although Jean acted as if she liked Bonnie, she also kept her distance as if she felt some kind of apprehension. Bonnie assumed it was because Jean's life was already full with classes and kids and there really wasn't time for any more friendships. A past-life regression would later explain that there had been more to the story.

Before the course was finished, Bonnie had to undergo back surgery for which she was admitted to the hospital. While there, she had a dream in which she purchased drinking glasses that had been engraved with her initials. She presented them to Jean, who looked at them and then told Bonnie that there just wasn't room for the glasses in her kitchen cabinet. In Bonnie's understanding, it suggested that Jean didn't think she had room for Bonnie in her life. The dream was very upsetting because Bonnie was still eager to form a friendship.

While Bonnie was still in the hospital, Jean came to visit. Sometime later, Bonnie decided to tell the dream to Jean and feign ignorance as to its meaning. After hearing it, Jean simply smiled and said, "Interesting." In the silence that followed, Bonnie was embarrassed but a moment later Jean spoke up and said, "I'm going out with some friends; how would you like to come with us?" At that moment, Bonnie knew that somehow Jean had decided to "make room" for her, after all. It was not long before the two women were very close, and within a short time they were working on creating and teaching adult education classes together.

A few years after the start of their friendship, Bonnie had a past-life regression that seemed to explain their connection as well as Jean's initial hesitancy to form a friendship. During the regression, Bonnie saw that the two had frequently been together in a variety of roles: teacher/student, teacher/teacher, and initiate/initiate. During one of those lifetimes, there had been an accident and she had been indirectly responsible for Jean's death. The accident was just one reason why Jean had been so hesitant to become friends in the present.

In another life, Bonnie saw that the two had trained

together as initiates at a time when she had apparently misjudged Jean. At that time, she felt that Jean was teaching the other initiates her own personal beliefs rather than spiritual truths. During the regression, Bonnie realized that she had a choice to make:

> I had three choices from my discovery: I could tell Jean what I was thinking, giving her a chance to tell me what was really happening; I could tell the head master of my suspicions; or I could do nothing. In the regression I knew that I had done nothing. As a result, I was not allowed to be a teacher of initiates because I had failed the test which had been given to me by the head master, and I was sent away . . .

Later, Bonnie would also have a "waking vision" in which she saw herself and Jean as teachers among an ancient people. In addition to confirming that she had something to share with others, the experience made her understand why she had been so drawn to teaching with Jean in the first place.

Since that time, Jean and Bonnie have taught hundreds of classes and workshops together. But more than simply being co-workers, they have become intimately connected as friends. Even though they admit to having differences from time to time, the magic of working together has never changed. Bonnie states, "Our combined creativity still excites both of us. The one thing unchanged in our relationship over the years is our unconditional acceptance and love of each other."

When Bonnie went through a traumatic divorce, it was Jean who gave her the courage and the means to get away. Afterward, Bonnie felt burned out and wanted to isolate herself from the outside world. Jean, however, kept bringing her back with the rationale of needing her for a lecture or workshop.

Their relationship has also been filled with joy and laughter. Bonnie explains:

In our years of working together, we have laughed and played like children, all the time creating classes, workshops, and projects that have been extremely helpful to others. Our friendship has endured over the years through personal challenges and difficulties as well as through times of great joy and excitement. We have supported each other and come to the other's defense. We never grow tired of working together or simply talking. We have a rare rapport that others often recognize and envy. For myself, I have found this relationship to be one of the main sources of my own life force. I have called it a transcendental relationship, with a love and acceptance that go beyond the realm of this lifetime.

In a final example from the Cayce readings, a seventeen-year-old college freshman named Randy was told that one of his best friends at the university had been associated with him in at least four previous lifetimes (78-1). In the present, he and his friend, Gus, often discussed philosophy and comparative religions. They enjoyed studying and simply hanging out together and found occasion to defend one another to other friends and associates. It was apparent that their soul mate relationship from the past was having a tremendous influence upon the present.

In their most recent lifetime together, the two had been monks in England and had spent many hours in study and deep contemplation. From that experience, both Randy and Gus had acquired a love of personal reflection and contemplation. During a lifetime at the height of the Crusades, Randy had been a shield-bearer and had died while defending his city's leader, who had reincarnated as Gus. From that experience, the two felt a need to defend their principles and friendships "at any cost." In an earlier lifetime as Christian missionaries, both Randy and Gus had ministered together and had suffered martyrdom because of their beliefs. In spite of their deaths, each still possessed a strong desire to study, discuss, and share with others information about spiritual truths.

In another lifetime, Randy had been Gus's younger brother in ancient Egypt. Although the two were originally at odds and on opposing sides during a political upheaval in the country, Randy eventually switched allegiances and became his brother's greatest ally and assistant. From that experience, each had learned to withhold judgment or criticism about another person until the facts spoke for themselves.

Over the next several years, Randy and Gus remained the best of friends. However, as is often the case in soul mate friendships, events caused the two to be separated by life's changes and geography. As each was led in different directions, enabling them to fulfill their individual life's purposes (and the accompanying job changes, marriages, moves, and children), they remained in contact by occasional letter for nearly twenty-five years. At some point after that time, they lost track of one another. In the files of the Cayce archives, no information is available on Randy after 1949 and Gus reportedly died sometime in the early 1980s, and yet their relationship is not over. Inevitably, Randy and Gus will pick up their ongoing connection to one another the next time they cross paths in space and time.

# 5

## *Soul Mate Groups and the Cycle of Reincarnation*

. . . we should clearly recognize that at the moment we meet someone with whom we are linked the element of destiny is at an end, and we are both from that time onward on our own. All that stems from our relations with one another in our previous lives remains to be worked out in this (and even subsequent) lives. We are able to act freely because at this stage of historical development we are in our waking life unaware of the details of our earlier relationship, and this enables us to come to totally fresh insights in this life, based on our perception of one another as we are now.

Rudolf Steiner
*Man and World in the*
*Light of Anthroposophy*

In addition to soul mate connections between individuals and among families, the Edgar Cayce readings make it clear that there are larger soul groupings to which individuals are drawn. These soul mate groups often manifest when individuals come together to create a larger work; for example, the faculty that makes up a university, the people who join one another in a unified cause; even the politicians, leaders, and citizens that create a country. Although these larger soul mate groupings appear to be secondary to a soul's individual lessons, they still have a tremendous impact upon the people involved as well as the broader world community.

In a reading (3976-29) given in 1944 during World War II, Cayce gave a couple of examples of soul mate groups which were being born into specific countries and would have an important influence upon the rest of the world. He stated that although "It will take years for it to be crystallized . . . " one day Communism would come to an end because souls had been purposefully choosing to be born in Russia with the ideal of freedom. In terms of another soul grouping, Cayce cited China and explained that many souls were being born with the goal of bringing religious freedom to the country. To be sure, the result would be "far off as man counts time," but he promised that a time would come when China would become "the cradle" of applied personal spirituality.

In addition to these positive examples, apparently soul groups also come together for negative purposes, such as religious and racial strife and prejudice. These negative patterns of behavior remain a part of the soul until the individual learns otherwise and the patterns are transformed. The readings make it clear that regardless of how long it may take, eventually each individual will be prompted to overcome these negative behaviors through a series of personal life experiences.

Soul mate groups within the cycle of reincarnation also become evident in many of the life readings given to individuals who were personally associated with Edgar Cayce. When he gave a reading dealing with an individual's past lives, Cayce repeatedly stated he was only drawing upon those incarnations that were having the biggest influence upon the present. In other words, the reading was not necessarily citing all of an individual's past lives, only those which were relevant to the person's present cycle. However, because a number of people were closely connected to Edgar Cayce's work in the present, it was not unusual for many of those same individuals to have been associated with him in the past. Cayce himself was so impressed with the interconnectedness between himself and so many others that he told one woman that if they ever had time to compile all of the information regarding how these groups of people had repeatedly been drawn together, "What a story it will make . . . " (Case 951-4 Report File).

In Edgar Cayce's own life readings (294-8 and others), he frequently discussed two past-life experiences for himself which were very influential in the present: one in ancient Egypt and another in ancient Persia. In Egypt he had been a high priest who had dispersed information about spiritual truths throughout the country. In ancient Persia, he had been a desert nomad who had founded a city that eventually became an important healing center. Apparently, many individuals had been influenced by his work during those periods in history, and a number of the very same individuals were being brought back together in the present. This soul mate group connection first became evident in 1928.

During that year Cayce gave a number of readings describing the purpose of the organization he had founded to explore and document his work.[5] Created primarily as

---

[5]Originally, the organization was called the Association of National Investigators (ANI). Later, in 1931, that organization was disbanded and reconstituted as the Association for Research and Enlightenment, Inc. (A.R.E.), which continues to serve as the international headquarters for the work of Edgar Cayce.

an educational institution with its own board, a staff, and interested members throughout the country, the goal of the organization was to disseminate the information contained in Cayce's psychic readings and to find ways of making the material applicable and practical in people's lives. While giving a reading to members of the organization, he made the surprising announcement that no individual would be drawn to or interested in the association they were creating "other than those that first established same in that land now known as Egypt" (254-42). Later readings confirmed the fact that the work they were establishing was the continuation of a similar work that many of the same individuals had begun thousands of years previously.

However, the group's unified desire to be part of an educational association in the present was not the only urge they had retained. Cayce suggested that many of these same individuals in the past had once opposed and even warred with one another in terms of how the work was to be accomplished. For that reason, at a soul level they would have similar frustrations, disagreements, and oppositions that needed to be met and overcome. The reading reminded the group to work together and to learn to cooperate with one another because "A divided house *cannot* stand."

During his lifetime, Cayce's organization brought together a number of smaller groupings of individuals in specific activities and functions. These activities included the founding of a hospital, the creation of a university, various research activities, and spiritually based discussion groups. When an ecumenical prayer group was established by the Association in 1931, a number of readings described how many of these same individuals had been a part of an identical group during the Egyptian period: "So we had the foundation of the Prayer Group" (281-42, 281-43, and others).

The group was told that as individuals they had been together in various juxtapositions, some positive and some negative, but as a group they had generally worked together for the common good of all. Cayce accurately predicted that in the present, as long as those individuals worked in a cooperative manner, eventually the group would have the opportunity to pray with *"thousands* of others" (294-127). Although all of the original members of the prayer group were deceased or had disbanded by the 1970s, the prayer group itself continued and by 1998 the group was sending out a monthly prayer list to approximately 4,000 individuals worldwide.

In terms of his Persian incarnation, one of Cayce's readings stated, "We find there are many upon this earth's plane, and in different locations, who were associated with this entity at that time" (294-8). Over the next twenty years, it appeared as though the reading had correctly anticipated a number of people who would be drawn back to the soul group because many of the life readings given to individuals during that same period discussed the importance of a Persian incarnation. In 1948, three years after his death, Cayce's secretary, Gladys Davis, compiled a listing of no less than fifty individuals who had received readings and had also been connected to Cayce's work in both Persia and Egypt (Case 294-153 Report File).

One of the most stunning examples of an individual being drawn back to a previous soul mate group is told in the bestselling book *The Search for Omm Sety* by Jonathan Cott. Published in 1987, Cott tells the story of Dorothy Eady, who was completely drawn to the world of the Egyptians rather than her birthplace of England. Somehow the memory of a previous soul mate group impacted her to such a degree that the past became more important than the present.

Dorothy Eady was born on January 16, 1904, in England and appeared to be a normal child in all respects. At the age of three, however, she fell down a flight of stairs and remained unconscious. Dorothy's mother summoned the family doctor, who, after examining the little girl, declared the child dead of a brain concussion. Dorothy was laid to rest on her bed while the family gathered together to grieve in another part of the house.

To her family's great joy and surprise, an hour later Dorothy was found to be playing in her room, appearing completely normal. Soon thereafter, the child began talking continuously about dreams she was having of an enormous temple building with grand columns, surrounded by beautiful gardens. Frequently, she was also found to be crying for no apparent reason. Whenever her mother attempted to console her and ask the child what was wrong, inevitably Dorothy's tearful reply was that she wanted to go "home." When assured that she was home, Dorothy would cry all the more, stating that she didn't know where her home was, but that she wanted to be taken there.

At the age of four, Dorothy went with her parents to the British Museum. She seemed bored and withdrawn until they came to the Egyptian galleries. At the sight of the galleries, Dorothy became completely enthralled, running from place to place with wide-eyed enthusiasm, kissing the feet of the statues, and taking in all that she could see. When her parents insisted that the time had come to continue on their tour, Dorothy refused to budge from the exhibit. Finally, in bewilderment, Dorothy's family left her unattended for half an hour and continued their sightseeing tour of the museum. When they returned to get the child, however, Dorothy still refused to leave. When her mother tried to lift her, Dorothy exclaimed, "Leave me . . . these are my people!"

Later that same year, Dorothy received a child's illustrated encyclopedia. The book happened to contain a picture of the Rosetta stone, which fascinated her. Because she so frequently stared at the stone, eventually her mother told her that the language was one that she couldn't possibly understand. Dorothy replied that she did indeed know the language; she had simply forgotten it.

At the age of seven while going through some of her father's magazines, Dorothy came across a photograph of an ancient Egyptian temple. To her amazement, it was a picture of the very same temple she had always dreamed about as a child: the temple of Sety the First of Abydos, Pharaoh of the Nineteenth Dynasty. Although the photo was of an archaeological dig and Dorothy's dreams were of a temple at its height, she recognized it immediately. Overjoyed by her discovery, Dorothy ran to her father and showed him the picture, shouting, "This is my home! This is where I used to live!"

Soon afterward, Dorothy came across a photograph of the extraordinarily well-preserved mummy of Sety the First. She excitedly explained to her father that she had known the man in the picture and that he had been exceedingly nice and kind. Frustrated to the breaking point, her father shouted back that she couldn't possibly have known the man since he had been dead for nearly 3,000 years. With that, Dorothy ran to her room, sobbing.

Undoubtedly, her parents thought she would outgrow her "imaginary" fantasies of Egypt. However, that day never came. At ten, Dorothy caught the eye of Sir E.A. Wallis Budge, a famous British Egyptologist who had observed the girl frequent the museum. At her insistence, he began helping her "remember" the hieroglyphic symbols. In a very short time she became adept enough to actually translate excerpts from the *Egyptian Book of the Dead*.

The dreams of Egypt became even more vivid, and Dorothy began seeing herself as a young Egyptian girl.

At times she would see herself in an underground cham-
ber surrounded by water. Interestingly, and unbeknownst to Dorothy at the time, to this day behind Sety's
temple in Abydos evidence survives of a large subterra-
nean hall in the middle of which existed a raised island
surrounded by water.

Her dreams persisted with greater detail—nightmares
in which Dorothy found herself as a young Egyptian girl
named Bentreshyt, being beaten with a stick by a severe-
looking high priest who had disapproved of something
she had done. She would later discover that Bentreshyt
and Sety the First had accidentally crossed paths, fallen
in love, and had had an affair.

From Dorothy's late teens into her twenties, she felt as
though she were simply waiting for the time when she
could return to Egypt. At the age of twenty-seven, she
got a job for an Egyptian public relations magazine,
through which she eventually met and married a young
man from an upper middle class family in Cairo. Finally,
in 1933, she took a boat to Port Said in Egypt in order to
join her fiancé. Upon reaching land, she knelt down,
kissed the ground, and swore never to leave her native
country again. She was twenty-nine years old and felt as
if she had finally come home. Although her goal was to
eventually reach Sety's temple in Abydos, she had at least
made it to Egypt.

From the very first, Dorothy's marriage was difficult.
She longed for the Egypt of the past, the monuments,
and a simpler time. Her husband, on the other hand,
liked the modern world. He wanted to be near the
middle and upper classes and he desired a wife—not an
Egyptologist. After having a son whom Dorothy insisted
on calling Sety, the couple eventually separated and divorced.

Dorothy got a job with the Egyptian Antiquities Department as a draftsperson at the site of the Great Pyra-

mid and the Sphinx. Though she longed to go to Abydos, she was content with her work assisting Egyptologists at the Giza plateau. Although known to be a bit eccentric at times, Dorothy was also regarded as a respected Egyptologist. She is credited with having written or coauthored several important works of Egyptology, as well as numerous articles, essays, and commentaries.

Because she was the mother of Sety, in proper Egyptian custom she became known as "Omm Sety." Although she made a couple of day trips to the city, it wasn't until 1956, at the age of fifty-two, that she finally moved to Abydos. For the next twenty-five years, until her death in 1981, Omm Sety helped to restore much of Abydos to its original grandeur. The attachment Dorothy Eady felt to the past had no explanation in the present and could have only come from somewhere deep within her soul.

A contemporary account of a soul mate group being drawn back together is told in the story of four individuals who all ended up working in both theater and human services. The story begins with Tom, who was director of an academy of performing arts. In 1987, while putting together the plays to be performed that season, Tom hired Kathleen to be one of his directors. Interestingly enough, he hired her "sight unseen" because of her previous directing experience as well as her education and background in theater. After Kathleen was hired, she held auditions for the play *The Good Doctor*. Because Kathleen was so impressed by one of the women, Lori, who had answered the casting call, she rewrote a male character's role so that Lori could be involved in the production. From that day on, Tom, Kathleen, and Lori would be involved in many theatrical performances together.

In July of that year, Kathleen took a full-time job working in a group home for mentally retarded adults. In her spare time, she maintained her involvement in theater as well as her connection with Lori and Tom. The three had become extremely close friends. Later in the year, when Tom needed more work, he also got a job in the group home. When Lori decided to go to nursing school the following year, she took a job in the group home as well to help finance her education. In spite of their respective families and their independent and busy schedules, the three continued to work together in human services and theater.

In 1989, when the group home needed to fill a vacant staff position, Lori suggested Janet, one of the individuals she had befriended at school. Shortly after being hired in human services, Tom asked Janet to take part in *Amadeus*, the group's most recent production. From that day forward, the group became four individuals—all committed to one another as friends, as co-workers involved in helping mentally retarded adults live "as normal lives as possible," and as individuals deeply drawn to theater and the performing arts.

To be sure, there were arguments and occasional jealousies among the four of them. Just because a relationship is between soul mates does not mean that there won't be problems. One problem that occurred was the fact that Kathleen and Lori often felt that Tom went out of his way to support and defend Janet, as if he needed to "take care of her." However, in spite of any disagreements, the group remained closely connected and continued to work and perform together. In time, in order to help the mentally retarded residents become even more involved in "normal society," Tom obtained permission from the human services agency to begin allowing some of the residents to work in various capacities at the theater.

Eventually, Kathleen obtained a psychic reading and inquired about the past-life connections within the group. The psychic told her that in addition to the group connection—a connection that extended to many additional individuals in the theater as well as some of the residents in the group home—all of the individuals involved had experienced relationships with one another independent of the group. For example, it was stated that Kathleen and Lori had been together as Native Americans, and three of the four had been united as a family in Egypt. When the individuals came together as a group, however, it was for a meaningful work. Examples of their united efforts were traced to Atlantis, Greece, and England.

In Atlantis the four had been involved with healing, the arts, intuition, and the dissemination of spiritual truths. At the time, they had been very interested in helping individuals with healing and tapping into their own inner creativity. The same group had been brought together in Greece at a time when they had created and performed their own pieces. Trained in the performing and musical arts, many of their performances portrayed humanity's relationship to the gods, as well as such concerns as philosophy and the dynamics of free will and fate. Their goal was to educate the public through the use of the arts.

The most recent group connection had been in London around the nineteenth century. At that time, Kathleen had been born into the lower classes and had scraped together a living as best she could. Because of her poverty, sometimes she was forced to prostitute herself. Eventually, a businessman appeared to take pity on her and hired her as a house servant. Unfortunately, the man's motives were not moral and he began to rape her and use her physically whenever he desired. It was a situation from which Kathleen was finally able to escape. A short time later, Kathleen was able to procure employment as a servant with an honest, wealthy nobleman.

That nobleman turned out to be Tom in the present.

Unfortunately, Kathleen's former employer was livid with jealousy and rage. Because of his connections, he was able to have Kathleen committed to an asylum for twenty-one days because of her reported "lack of morality." While she was there, Tom used his own connections to get the servant he felt compassion for released.

Because of Kathleen's personal experience in the asylum and Tom's visits to release her, the two saw the despicable conditions under which human beings were being mistreated. Regardless of their mental, emotional, or physical disabilities, people were thrown together without concern for their treatment or welfare. Abuse of all kinds was common. Some of the residents were caged; others were naked, lying in their own waste. It was a depravity of human existence that neither Tom nor Kathleen had ever imagined. From that day forward, they vowed to do something about it.

Tom's nineteenth-century counterpart turned part of his estate into a residence where the mentally and physically disabled could "live as normally as possible." Kathleen started working for Tom in that endeavor. Residents were given fresh air, clean clothing, and good nutrition. They received appropriate medical treatment as well. In time, some of the residents, who might have spent their lifetime committed in the regular asylum, could be treated and eventually released. Lori's nineteenth century counterpart became involved because her daughter had been committed to an asylum. After witnessing the horrendous conditions, Lori pulled her daughter out of the state institution and put her in the residence that Tom had begun. Tom's present-day support and attachment to Janet was traced to the fact that she had been his daughter in that nineteenth-century existence and would later continue the legacy of helping the mentally disadvantaged that he had begun.

In the present, all the information seemed relevant to Kathleen but what she found most interesting was the fact that in this life, three out of four in the group had once had individuals from their own families in a mental hospital for one reason or another. Once again, the group had been brought together for healing, creativity, and helping those less fortunate than themselves. Later, two of the group's members would continue to expand their commitment to the mentally disadvantaged. Just as he had done in the nineteenth century, Tom would turn part of his farm into a home where the mentally disabled could live normal lives, and Lori would become a psychiatric nurse.

The Edgar Cayce readings suggest that souls are destined to be drawn back together to groups and activities with which they have been previously associated. Some of these groups have been a helpful influence; others have been less than positive. However, what is certain is—as Cayce told one individual—"no associate *ever* becomes a part of thine experience save as an opportunity for the developing of that thou dost hold as thy ideal" (1581-2). In other words, in spite of what might have occurred in the past, all of our relationships can become a purposeful experience in the present as long as we keep foremost in mind the ultimate purpose for being in the earth, which is simply to manifest the law of love.

# 6

## Challenges in Soul Mate Relationships

There can never be a perfect world unless gradually
those born into it can take advantage of lessons learned
in earlier lives instead of starting at scratch.

Leslie D. Weatherhead, Ph.D.
*The Case for Reincarnation*

Regardless of one's challenges in life, the Edgar Cayce readings make it clear that the soul draws to it those difficulties and opportunities which might best enable it to "meet self." As a result, every relationship has its share of challenges. Rather than seeing problems as being external to one's self, Cayce believed that each individual was somehow an integral cocreator in the unfolding process of her or his life's journey. Ultimately, there is no such thing as a "victim," unless an individual chooses to respond as such. All of life's challenges and opportunities have the potential to be of great assistance in the process of spiritual growth and personal transformation.

In 1939 Edgar Cayce was presented with an interesting case of a "relationship triangle" that illustrates the dynamics of three people truly having the opportunity to meet themselves. The case involved a forty-nine-year-old woman, Mae, who came with her husband, Howard, as well as "the other woman" to get a reading about a situation that had developed—an affair of the heart. She told Mr. Cayce that her husband and the other woman were "so much in love they don't know what to do." Since her husband was physically impotent, Mae knew that the attraction wasn't physical in nature, but she was in tears and at her wits' end about how to understand or cope with the situation.

Earlier readings had placed the husband and wife together at least three times previously, in Palestine, Egypt, and Persia. In Persia, Mae had used her influence and selfishness to place herself above those around her. During that same period, her husband had apparently been quite prolific sexually and had surrounded himself with "too many wives in that experience for his own good!" (289-9). According to the reading, it was the lifetime in Persia that had helped to create the current situation. Evidently, the present-day girlfriend had been one of Howard's wives and Mae had somehow used her position against the other woman. As a result, each of the three was now "meeting themselves."

Cayce advised the threesome that Howard and Mae were "Needed as a helpmeet one for the other." In terms of his relationship with the other woman, the husband was told to "make it a beautiful thing, and not something ugly!" (413-11). Because the man had loved both women previously, that love continued at a soul level, but it needed to be made appropriate for the current situation. In order to determine their future course of action, the reading recommended that each constantly ask themselves, "What would ye have thy God say? What would ye have thy children say? What would ye have thy neighbor say?"

The three individuals were told that the situation was a great learning experience and could become a "stepping-stone" in their individual growth rather than the difficulty it appeared to be. Each was encouraged to keep the feelings of the other two in mind: "live, act towards each in the same manner as ye would that each would act towards thee if conditions were reversed." Each was also told to not blame or condemn the other two—the situation was to be met in unconditional love.

After the reading, Mae tried her best to follow the reading's advice. After some time, she requested another reading on her own and inquired as to how well she was dealing with the situation. Cayce told her, "few are making such headway, such strides even, in manifesting patience and love" (413-13). The reading ended with a note of hope for the wife: "Hold fast to that faith. For, the day dawns for more peace, more harmony, more happiness in thy experience."

Shortly thereafter, Howard and the other woman broke off their attachment to each other and Mae and Howard were able to resume their marriage. Even after Howard began to suffer from heart problems a few years later, his wife continued to take care of him and love him. Perhaps most of all, she had overcome whatever selfishness remained at a soul level and truly learned the lesson of unconditional love. Howard passed away in 1968. No mention of the other woman is contained within the report files. Mae, however, lived a long and productive life, surrounded by family and friends until her own death in 1991 at the remarkable age of 101.

Another family challenge is explored in the case of a thirty-one-year-old woman and her husband who obtained a joint reading about their difficult relationship. Both individuals were on their second marriage and both wanted to know how they could overcome some of the marital problems they were presently facing. In addition to many disagreements, one of the couple's problems was an ongoing animosity between the husband and the woman's son from her first marriage. Cayce told the couple that it wasn't by chance that the entire family had come together, rather it was for the material, mental, and spiritual development of all concerned. They were encouraged not to reject the opportunity they had been given to grow with each other. There were many reasons for staying together whereas the only reason for separating would be because of self and selfishness. When the woman asked, "Why are we so uncomfortable with one another?" Cayce replied:

They each have made up their mind they don't care and they don't like to be together; yet if they will analyze—together—those problems of each that have existed, and try—*try*—to meet them on a common basis, the situation will be understood and the uncomfortableness will be erased. 263-18

When the couple asked how they could feel more married, the advice was "By making the purposes of each as one." Another question was, "Why is it so hard for us to agree on anything?" The response was, "Each looks for the differences, rather than that on which ye *can* agree!" In addition to looking at one another differently, they were advised to find some activity, hobby, or recreation they could all agree upon and do together. In terms of the overall relationship between the three, it was emphasized that each must learn to *"Minimize the faults, magnify the virtues!"* Finally, Cayce encouraged the couple to "so live, so act, one toward the other, as to make this experience—here and now—worth while!"

Difficulties between them continued and by 1944 the couple had separated. However, the separation was brief and they decided to reconcile. According to the reports on file, not only did the husband and wife really attempt to work together, but the man's relationship with his stepson also improved. In time, friends noted that the couple "did a wonderful job of making their marriage work." Their married and home life became an inspiration to many. The relationship continued until the woman's death in July 1963. When the husband finally died of a heart attack in 1967, his stepson stated that in every respect the man had become "a real father" to him.

In another case of a relationship triangle, over a two-and-a-half-year period a thirty-four-year-old New York attorney, [2052], obtained several readings regarding his relationship with two women: his wife and his girlfriend to whom he felt hopelessly drawn. In the man's own words, "I seem to love them both in different ways and don't want to injure either one."

Cayce told the man that his situation was identical to one he had experienced as a member of a Jewish tribe during the time of Moses. At that time, [2052] had been married to his present wife and had been caught in adultery with his present girlfriend. The punishment for adultery had been death and the man and his girlfriend were swiftly executed. In the present, the situation had come together again and he was encouraged to overcome his attraction to his girlfriend and to fulfill the commitment to his wife he had once forsaken. Cayce stated that the man's attraction to his girlfriend was based primarily on desire and self-gratification whereas his relationship with his wife had a much greater potential: "There *are* those possibilities of this becoming a union in which *both* may become *real* helpmates one for the other" (2052-2).

In spite of the advice he received in two readings, in 1941 the man ran away from his wife, obtained a Mexican divorce (invalid in New York), and married his girlfriend. A few months later, he felt guilty about leaving his first wife so he returned to her. After a few months of being back with his first wife, he left her and returned to his second. In April of 1942, being more confused than ever before, [2052] requested a third reading and wondered what he was supposed to do about the whole situation. He also inquired as to whether or not the readings had ever recommended divorce.

During the course of the third reading, Cayce reminded [2052] that his attraction to his second wife was based primarily upon desire and self-gratification. The reading told the man that it would be far better for his second wife if he would let her go to pursue other relationships. He was also reminded that he had "belittled" his first wife in the past and that he was continuing to do so in the present. If he persisted along the same course, [2052] would further degrade himself and both women and possess "a continued consciousness of wrongdoing." He was strongly encouraged to follow the proper course of action.

Although the readings had recommended divorce in other cases for several reasons, none of those reasons were applicable in [2052]'s situation. Essentially, the rationale for divorce included: (1) when an individual was in danger of physical, mental, or spiritual harm by remaining with the other; (2) where two people had truly overcome what required to be worked out together; or (3) where one individual had overcome the lesson and the other refused to.

In January 1946, [2052] sent a follow-up report to the Cayce Foundation. He stated that he had returned to his second wife and had fathered one child. Eventually guilt overcame him and he returned to his first wife but their final reconciliation had been short-lived. He was now convinced that he had never truly loved either woman; understandably, neither of his wives wanted anything further to do with him.

Mr. [2052] went on to state that he was in the midst of extreme depression and emotional instability. He also believed that, in the summer of 1945, he had finally found his true soul mate. From her, he had been "truly spiritually awakened to the true meaning of love." Although he was then thirty-nine and she was only twenty-one: "Perfect companionship was our mutual experience, and we became wholly lost in one another. In music, literature, and art, we found the same emotional interest. Two people could not have loved each other more." Unfortunately, the woman was married to another man and [2052] himself had never actually obtained a valid divorce. Nonetheless, for the next few months, the couple continued their relationship. On Christmas Day, both of their present spouses finally consented to divorces. Tragically, [2052]'s younger girlfriend was stricken with an attack of diabetes later that same day and died within seventy-two hours. The whole situation had left [2052] "so lonely and emotionally devastated that I have lost interest in life." Part of his reason for writing the follow-up report was to inquire if his pain was due to his own choices. He also wondered where he might look to find someone similar to the love of his life that he had lost.

Gina Cerminara, a member of the office staff, replied to [2052]'s letter and told him to "forget about finding another woman for the time being." He was advised to begin helping others in service and to cultivate love within himself to share selflessly rather than looking for someone to love him. He was sent information from the readings regarding the purpose of life and encouraged to become more selfless in his activities. By August of that year, [2052] wrote once again. He was making strides in the healing process and wanted to thank Gina for the information she had sent: "It has served greatly to enrich my life and to thwart the self-indulgence and self-gratification of which I was said to be subject." Although [2052] remained interested in Cayce's organization until the 1960s, there is no additional information on file as to whether or not he ever married again.

An interesting example of the turnabout of past-life retribution is told in the story of Mr. [953]. According to Cayce, in ancient Egypt, [953] had once banished a married man for running off with another woman. Without regard to possible reasons for the situation, apparently [953] had simply followed the letter of the law. Being forced to leave Egypt had nearly devastated the banished man.

The situation played out in the present, because in spite of a bad marriage situation [953]'s wife refused to grant him a divorce. Appearing to have no other option, eventually [953] left his wife, took a common-law wife, and had two sons by the second woman. He very much loved the second woman and wanted to legally marry her but was never able to do so. The whole situation caused [953] much regret and personal pain, but it was simply in recompense for having unjustly punished someone for something he would eventually do himself.

In August 1942 a woman asked about the past-life connection between herself and her boyfriend. She was told that he had been her companion several times previously and that the two were especially connected because of a lifetime in India. At that time, the woman had gained spiritually because of her ability to help others. During the same incarnation, however, she had lost spiritually due to her own "self-indulgence." As far as the relationship with her boyfriend was concerned, the two of them had vastly different opinions about many things but if they chose to work together they could "do well by such associations in the present." On the other hand, if they were not careful, they would become "stumbling forces" in each other's lives. According to follow-up reports, within seven years the couple had married and divorced (2800-2).

A young man was told that he and his wife had been together several times previously. In their most recent lifetime together, the wife had been much older and she had been hired as the governess and nanny to her present husband. They had also been together in a previous marriage relationship in which the two had failed to learn how to work with each other. They had come together again to be given a second chance. Cayce told the man, "They were *not* successful in their former association." For the soul growth of all concerned, the reading added, "Make them so in the present . . . " Later reports suggest that they did learn to work together and eventually raised "three lovely daughters" (2167-1).

In 1937, a woman, [1483], requested a life reading in which she inquired why her boyfriend was so slow in making up his mind about getting married. Although there was a definite connection between the two, and she desperately wanted to get married, her boyfriend, [1173], seemed to constantly change his mind. Edgar Cayce traced the attraction between the two to an early American incarnation, when the woman had been the wife of the man's best friend. Apparently, at that time [1483] had been unfaithful to her husband and had an ongoing relationship with her present boyfriend, [1173]. Cayce told the woman that her longing to be with her boyfriend was not based on love but rather on the desire to possess him that she had created during that earlier incarnation. She was gently advised that there were others with whom her boyfriend would be much happier in the present, just as there were others with whom she could create a better marriage relationship.

One week later a joint reading was obtained for the couple, again inquiring about the prospect of a marriage between the two. Once again, Cayce stated that there was definitely an attraction between them as well as urges from the past that needed to be worked through in the present. He reminded the woman that she needed to work through her desire to have her own way and to possess [1173]. He told the man that the greatest past-life urge with which he was dealing was not the desire for home and marriage with [1483], but rather the innate feeling that the woman's life was missing something and that she needed someone to protect her. He told them that if they were to marry, "it would become a *burden* upon each" (1173-11).

Cayce reminded the two that they were simply meeting patterns that they had created previously: "They each are faced with *themselves!* It is nothing but themselves they are faced with!" Although they had the freedom of choice to decide what they should do about the situation, Cayce's advice was to learn to overcome the desires that had been created on the part of the woman because of "self-indulgence" and the part of the man because of "self-sacrifice." When [1173] asked what kind of a relationship the two should attempt to cultivate in the present, he was told, "friendship." The couple followed the advice and did not get married.

A contemporary example of successfully overcoming a situation that may have originated in a past life is told in the story of Alicia and James. They met in the 1950s when James was twenty-four and working for a trucking firm and Alicia was twenty and employed by a paper company. From the very first, there seemed to be some unresolved issue between them. According to Alicia, she saw James after she had gone to the coffee shop for her morning break:

> James came in for a cup of coffee while they unloaded his truck. I recognized him as a high school classmate's brother. I can remember very well

thinking how mad I was at him. I didn't want to get
married at twenty and I just *knew* I would marry
him. I was not ready for marriage. I remember getting very angry as we sat in the coffee shop that day.

Later James called her and asked for a date. In spite of
the fact that she did not want to get married just yet, Alicia agreed to go out with him. Her anger was renewed on
their second date when the fact that her Uncle Frank had
previously employed James was discussed. James told
her, "I never thought I would be related by marriage to
Frank!" The statement made Alicia feel "as mad as could
be" because she wasn't at all ready to get married. To
make matters worse, Alicia's mother was not at all happy
about her daughter's relationship with someone whom
the older woman considered unsuitable. She and her
mother continually fought about it. Then something
happened which made the entire situation even more
difficult: Alicia became pregnant by James.

In spite of her family problems, Alicia, by her own admission, was very emotionally tied to her mother. She
didn't know what to do or where to go. Her greatest fear
was that her mother would disown her. Although James
begged her to get married, Alicia was too scared. She was
also afraid to tell her mother that she was pregnant. Not
knowing where else to turn, Alicia went to Puerto Rico to
live with her sister and brother-in-law for several
months to sort things out. When she returned home, she
told her parents what had happened. They demanded
that she go to the Salvation Army's unwed mothers'
home, have the baby, give it up for adoption, and "never,
never let anyone know what happened."

Not strong enough to do anything else, Alicia followed
her parents' demands. She entered the unwed mothers'
home. Shortly thereafter, she became dangerously ane-
mic, and the doctors placed her in the hospital to dis-

cover the reason. Proving that her anger had not abated, Alicia's mother stated that the reason for the anemia was not important and if her daughter bled to death during the delivery it would be "God's work" and "a blessing." Her mother assured her that she would rather see Alicia "dead than have an illegitimate child." Alicia eventually regained her health and had a baby girl, but Alicia's mother refused to acknowledge the child.

After her baby's birth, Alicia knew that she could never give up the child. She contacted James and the two arranged to pick up the baby and begin their life together as a family. For a long while, Alicia's mother remained bitter and angry about the situation. James and Alicia married, and within a few years they had a second daughter. Alicia's father came to love James and enjoyed being with him, but her mother remained distant and "stand-offish" for the rest of her life.

About ten years after their marriage, Alicia had a vivid dream that suggested her relationship with James had previously come to an abrupt end during the Civil War:

> We were in the South, and I knew it was the Civil War period. We were at a big, beautiful mansion where an orchestra with many violins was playing and the people were waltzing. I was standing outside the mansion with a young man. When I looked at him, I was very surprised at how different James looked in that life, but I knew it was he. He was a very young boy who, I felt, was going to war. He had a uniform on and was carrying either a sword or a gun. I was dressed in a full ball gown that ballooned out with petticoats and pantaloons. I decided to run across the grass, jump over a short hedge, and run into the woods. He looked shocked, turned his head in all directions to see if anyone were watching, and then ran after me into the woods. In the dream, I

felt that shortly thereafter he had gone to war and died as a young boy. I knew that we were together in the present lifetime to fulfill our marriage.

Interestingly enough, throughout their life together, James and Alicia have both been intensely drawn to the Civil War period.

Years later, when Alicia obtained a psychic reading, the psychic told her that in a previous life she had been abandoned by her parents and had become pregnant out-of-wedlock. During that lifetime, the pregnancy had caused her a great deal of grief and bitterness, and she had become very religious as a means of seeking forgiveness. The psychic told her that she had never really forgiven herself, so it was important for Alicia to learn how to truly love and forgive herself in this lifetime.

During the early years of her marriage to James, Alicia had a serious health problem which caused her to experience a great deal of anger and resentment. Regardless of how mad she became or how frequently she "lashed out" at her husband, his love remained steadfast. Working through that experience with her husband's unconditional love and her children's love and support became instrumental in helping Alicia learn to love herself.

In reflecting on the present-life situation, Alicia realizes that there was a possibility she might have decided not to get together with James. To be sure, it would have been a mistake. What is interesting about the possibility is that after their daughter's birth, the child had a severe case of dysentery and needed immediate medical attention. According to Alicia, "I have wondered many times if her soul would have chosen to leave if she knew that she would not be in the environment which included James and me. I am ever thankful to my Creator that we made the decision to stay together."

After nearly forty years of marriage, James and Alicia

have learned a great deal from each other. She tends to be very emotional and sensitive; he is very objective and thoughtful. She enjoys being with all kinds of people; James is the type that can be very content by himself or with members of their family. From Alicia's perspective, James has always possessed an inner strength. He seems to be at peace with himself. He is happy with who he is, as well as with his talents and limitations. His example has helped Alicia learn a great deal about herself. Alicia believes they have learned to find "balance" in their lives by being with one another.

Throughout their marriage, the couple have shared a deep commitment to their two children and shared the same family values. They provided the girls with an environment of love, nurturing, support, and trust:

> When raising our two girls, we met our challenges with complete trust in them. No matter what happened, we had total trust that they would do the best they could do, we would support them in it, and we would help in anyway possible. Our daughters were growing up when there were big challenges for them, i.e., drugs, alcohol, sex, etc. When they were adults, we asked them how they were able to grow up around all of that, but not get involved with it. They both said simultaneously that they knew we had so much trust in them and they just couldn't let us down.

The couple's support and love for their children has continued even though their daughters are grown. Recently, their youngest daughter has gone through a traumatic and devastating marriage and divorce. She is now the single mother of three, and Alicia and James have put their retirement and travel plans on hold to help their daughter financially and help her with the children. During the day, the couple watch their grandchildren; rather than seeing it as a burden, "we both feel it is a blessing from God to have these three souls so involved with us."

To this day, James and Alicia share a mutual respect and admiration for one another. To their friends and family, they appear to be "joined at the hip" and have become a shining example of a couple deeply committed to their relationship. Some have commented that their marriage seems as if it were "made in heaven." Alicia believes that her relationship with James has been "the greatest gift of my life" and has helped her to experience what a soul mate relationship truly entails:

> He has been my angel in the earth—an ever-present help in trouble. He has been my greatest spiritual teacher and support. A soul mate relationship is a deep bond that is unbreakable and irreplaceable. It is an inner knowing that this person is someone special sent into your life to cherish, experience things with, and share things together. It is not always a smooth, happy road, but the bond is there no matter what the pitfalls or experiences may be. Patterns can be detected and made stronger or changed because of the bond that you have. Lessons can be learned and spiritual growth takes place. I feel that it is not so important what happens to you in life but how you decide to deal with what happens to you.

Another example of challenges in soul mate relationships from the Cayce files is evident in the story of two women who came together as college roommates in 1932. Each was lonely and desperately craved to be married and have a family. One of the women, [369], had carried on an unhappy love affair with a man that had gone nowhere for a number of years. The other woman,

[1922], often felt responsible for her friend's state of mind. A reading (369-16) stated that the two women had often been associated before and could truly be of help to one another in the present. They were encouraged to use their connection to help each other "work out her own purposes." They could be a creative influence in the lives of others; however, they could also abuse their connection. Apparently, they could use their soul mate relationship to either assist or hinder one another in their respective life journeys.

Over a period of twenty years, the two women sent follow-up reports to the Cayce Foundation. After a brief stint at college, the two women separated as roommates and attempted to find husbands. The two stayed in communication through correspondence and frequent visits. From the reports on file, whenever one of the women found happiness with a possible relationship, the other became depressed and withdrawn because her friend had finally found someone whereas she had not. In one of the file notations from the 1930s, Gladys Davis wrote:

> Perhaps Miss [1922] would have married except for that fact that Miss [369] was so lonely and unhappy that Miss [1922] could not bring herself to make dates; she did not want to make her suffer by knowing that her friend was being "fulfilled" while she wasn't. Case 1922-1 Report File

After a period of years, friends of each warned them about continuing their dependence upon the other. Some wondered whether or not the two women might be homosexual, but each claimed she was not interested in a physical relationship. They simply had a strong "mental-emotional" connection. Regardless of the reasons for their connection, it became obvious to outsiders that each seemed incapable of making a decision independent of the other. To make matters worse, Miss [369] often came in contact with the man with whom she had once had an affair. She continued to be drawn to him and scared about the possibility of renewing the relationship. She became extremely anxious and depressed and eventually obtained a "prefrontal lobectomy" to help ease her fears.

The women remained friends and were frequently in the other's company, even though they didn't always live together. Their joint unhappiness at not being able to find a mate continued. At some point both women became heavily addicted to alcohol and tranquilizers. Years later, when Miss [369] got married to someone much younger than herself after a brief engagement, Miss [1922] became so upset that she became ill and had to move back home with her parents. When [369]'s husband moved to another city and waited for his wife to join him, [369] became so emotionally torn between her commitment to her friend or following after her husband that she killed herself.

Sadly, after her friend's death, [1922] admitted that she would always miss [369], but that the turn of events had probably been "for the best." No additional reports are on file. Throughout their soul mate connection, it appears as though the two women abused their relationship by holding the other back rather that using it to help each fulfill her respective purpose in life, as had been the original intention.

A communication issue seemed to be the biggest challenge in the relationship of Tracy and Michael. Although they had instantly "connected" and been drawn to one another, as soon as they were together, they seemed to argue about everything. It was not unusual for the couple to have fights five or six times a week! The fights included everything from staying together or splitting up to arguments about bills and money, as well as confrontations about their different communication styles. For the first few years of their relationship, it often appeared as though the couple were destined to break up. However, in spite of their ongoing challenges with one another, there seemed to be a deep connection between them.

At Tracy's insistence, the couple, now married, began to undergo individual and joint therapy sessions. The focus of the therapy was for them to learn to communicate. Among other issues, Michael needed to be more open and learn how to share his feelings. He also needed to become less self-sufficient and more cooperative with his wife. In addition to issues of self-esteem, Tracy needed to quit responding to Michael as though he had complete control over their lives. Both individuals needed to perceive the other as "an equal." After a few months of therapy, the arguments between them began to lessen considerably. Although they still fought two or three times a week, both of them realized that they were no longer fighting every day.

As part of their therapy, Tracy underwent several past-life regression sessions. Those same past lives were later discussed when the couple received a psychic reading about their relationship. In one of their lives together, they had been members of a large nomadic tribe. At the time, Michael had been Tracy's father; Tracy had been Michael's son. The period was a time of great political upheaval and change. The father had chosen to sit and wait things out—praying that God would take care of the situation. Conversely, the son had decided to take matters into his own hands and become a part of a military revolution. Although their styles of handling the situation had been vastly different, each shared the same problem in that the society of which they were a part was in the midst of great change.

The psychic informed the couple that, ultimately, nei-

ther of their responses to the situation had been correct.
Their lesson at the time had been to try to work together
and ask themselves, "Do we have the same problem and
ultimately do we have the same goal?" Together they
could have worked toward a common end rather than
becoming isolated from one another by their differing
responses. What the tribe had needed was a "revolution"
that mobilized the society as people, both socially and
politically.

The couple's communication issue had been repeated
in England where Michael and Tracy had been a married
couple. During that lifetime, Michael had a tendency to
communicate harshly, if at all, and Tracy often kept
things within herself. Tracy's family had left her a 600-
year-old estate—an estate that became Michael's "property" after their marriage. In time, Michael would use the
estate as collateral without Tracy's knowledge or con-
sent. Because of failed business dealings and unwise financial speculation, the entire estate was lost. Once
again, they shared the same problem, but neither wished
to deal with it. In time, the couple's English counterparts
withdrew even further from one another.

In the present, Michael and Tracy's relationship with
one another and their communication have continued
to improve. They have worked through many issues and
have found that whenever they work together, things
tend to run very smoothly. As one example, in spite of
the fact that many couples have problems when building a home, Michael and Tracy discussed everything
from the beginning of the floor plans to the end of con-
struction and "didn't even have one fight!" The experience required the dedication and financial commitment
of both individuals. After seven years, they have found
that rather than either of them being "in charge," theirs
is a relationship that "works best when we work together
and communicate with one another as equals."

A woman whose daughter and son-in-law were experiencing marital difficulties was reminded that her daughter's experience could be a purposeful one. In a Cayce reading she was told, "Individuals do not meet by chance. They *are* necessary in the experiences of others, though they may not always use their opportunities in a spiritual way or manner" (2751-1). The woman was advised not to interfere in the relationship and not to condemn anyone as being at fault either. Instead of attempting to solve her daughter's problems—which had been the woman's original intent—she was encouraged to aid her daughter as best she could without becoming personally involved. The daughter and her husband later divorced.

Cayce told another couple that their best opportunity for personal development came with being with each other. At the time of their meeting, the woman, [934], had just ended an unhappy first marriage. The man, [391], very much wanted to be married to her because he felt an almost overpowering pull toward her. In addition to other past-life connections, a reading traced the attraction between the couple to a lifetime in Greece. Shortly after the reading, they were married and had a child.

In spite of their immediate attraction, from the very first, the marriage unfortunately was difficult. Both were strong-willed and unyielding. Just two months after the marriage, the couple separated. Another reading was obtained in which Cayce told the couple that they could, in fact, work together. Apparently, there was an obligation that each owed the other from the past. Both needed to learn to be less willful and more able to compromise: "Each should be a complement one *to* the other. And this *can* be made true, if it will be worked together. It cannot be made true separated or apart!" (391-8). The couple was advised that they both needed to play a very important role in the raising of their son.

In spite of the advice, over the next ten years the couple reconciled and separated at least five times. During that same period, they were married to each other twice and divorced the same number of times. Eventually, they separated for good and married others from whom they also later divorced. Throughout all that time, their son had a very turbulent upbringing. Two decades later, in reflecting back upon her life, [934] stated that she wished she had been as wise twenty years earlier as she is today because she truly believes that she could have made her marriage to [391] work after all.

In a final contemporary example, a man fell in love and married a woman twenty years his junior. It was his second marriage and her first. The couple seemed very happy in many respects. After nearly ten years of being together, however, the woman became embarrassed by the fact that every once in awhile, when calling out to her husband, she would unconsciously yell out to him as "Dad." Understandably, every time it happened, she was horrified. For his part, the husband couldn't help but be reminded of their age difference. As time went on, the two developed more of a friendship than a marriage and they eventually divorced "as friends."

Without knowing the situation or the age difference, a psychic would later tell the husband that his ex-wife had most recently been his daughter during a lifetime as Indians in which the two had been "very close." Unfortunately, before even becoming a teenager, the daughter contracted an illness and died. It gave the man an eerie feeling of "coincidence" when the psychic informed him that his daughter had died at the age of twelve—the exact length of time he and his wife had been together as a couple.

# 7

## Twin Souls

I've spent my life looking for this woman, I thought. Told myself here's my mission, to be together with her again.

I was wrong. Finding her wasn't the object of my life, it was an imperative incident. Finding her allowed my life to begin.

Richard Bach
*The Bridge Across Forever*

One of the most complex and misunderstood topics in the area of relationships contained within the Cayce material is the concept of twin souls. Oftentimes, people have discussed the term as though it primarily suggests that two individuals who were separate halves of the same soul needed to find one another to become whole. With this in mind, individuals who received readings inevitably wanted to find their "other half" so they asked Edgar Cayce where they might find their twin soul or whether or not their current spouse or boyfriend/girlfriend was a "twin." Sometimes, these same individuals used such terms as "twin rays" or "twin flames" inter-changeably to describe the same thing.

In one instance, a twenty-seven-year-old woman who had been told of two past-life connections with her hus-band as Egyptians and as Incans wanted to know whether or not she and her husband were twin souls. Cayce replied, "That there are identical souls, no. No two leaves of a tree, no two blades of grass are the same" (3285-2). The reading went on to suggest that she and her husband were soul companions and could be complements to one another whenever they worked to-gether with a united purpose. More than anything else, this "unity of purpose" is what best describes Cayce's concept of what is at the heart of a twin soul relation-ship.

Rather than being primarily a sexual relationship or some kind of a romantic entanglement, the Cayce read-ings suggest that the focus of a twin soul relationship is one of shared ideals and purposes. Twin souls come to-gether in order to fulfill some important work that they have in common. Oftentimes that relationship mani-fests not as a romantic couple but as two people being brought together for a purposeful endeavor. The read-ings often pointed to various parent-child relationships as being that of twin souls. For example, Cayce stated that Jesus of Nazareth and his mother, Mary, were twin souls (5749-8 and others). Somehow, by being together, twin souls can assist one another in achieving their joint mission in life.

Although the focus of a twin soul relationship remains that of a shared work, it is possible for twin souls to come together in a specific lifetime as a couple. As to whether or not twin souls are separate halves of the same whole, the Cayce readings make it clear that all souls are indi-viduals and at the same time deeply connected to their Creator. This interconnection is so essential to the nature of the soul that ultimately every person is an individualized portion of the same Whole. Ultimately, a twin soul relationship is not "better" or more important than a relationship between soul mates. However, twin souls do appear to have a unique and ongoing influence upon one another throughout many of their incarnations in the earth. The soul stories of Edgar Cayce and some of those closest to him present an interesting case history of the twin soul phenomenon.

Perhaps more than any others, the lives of four individuals were responsible for the work that became the Edgar Cayce legacy: Edgar Cayce; his wife, Gertrude Cayce; his secretary, Gladys Davis; and his eldest son, Hugh Lynn Cayce. These four people came together to create an organization that would grow to be international in scope and do much to change the public's awareness of many subjects, including holistic health, reincarnation, dreams, spirituality, and psychic phenomenon.

Over the years, the readings verified that Edgar, Gertrude, Gladys, and Hugh Lynn were soul mates to one another as well as to many others. As a couple, Edgar and Gertrude shared a lifetime connection to each other that became evident to all those who knew them. During his life, Cayce had dreams that seemed to suggest their inevitable marriage as well as the fact that he and Gertrude probably would have died much sooner had they not come together as husband and wife.[6] In 1942, Edgar wrote the following inscription to his wife: "The promises of God always seem surer when I am with you—indeed a helpmate through this life." The readings also confirmed the fact that Edgar had a twin soul who would be instrumental in helping him to accomplish his work

---

[6]More details about the relationship between Gertrude and Edgar Cayce are discussed in chapter 1.

in this lifetime. However, his twin soul was identified not as Gertrude Cayce but as Gladys Davis. In a similar twist, Hugh Lynn and his mother were told that they were twin souls as well.

In some respects it may be impossible to discern between the outward appearance of a soul mate relationship and the coming together of twin souls. Soul mates and twin souls entail an ongoing connection between two individuals. Both kinds of relationships occur at the soul level, and both can be instrumental in assisting an individual in her or his spiritual growth. More importantly from Cayce's perspective, neither relationship is one which individuals need to go out and look for—these soul relationships will inevitably unfold during one's life. The primary distinction between soul mates and twin souls is that soul mates are brought together as a means of assisting both individuals in soul growth and twin souls often come together in an effort to achieve a joint task or a united work.

In an effort to demonstrate the ways in which soul mates and twin souls come together, the following is a brief overview of the past lives of the four individuals most responsible for the Cayce work in its formative years:

Hugh Lynn Cayce was told that he was very intelligent and had a deep love and respect for the work of Jesus. He was also a great builder of organizations and structures, loved contemplative study and pursuits of the mind, felt very much at home in the outdoors and nature, and was an effective communicator. Some of his most influential past lives included one as one of the first Pharaohs of Egypt, a contemporary follower and missionary of Jesus, a Bavarian warrior and Crusader, and a monk in England (341-1 and others). As a child, he often discussed his desire to be a missionary in China. Part of that desire was traced to the fact that he had once lived a very productive life in China at a time when he had been closely associated with his present wife, Sally. A soul mate connection between him and his wife was also traced to the period in Palestine when the two had been brother and sister.

Gertrude Cayce possessed innate talents as both an artist and a dancer. While Edgar Cayce had worked as a photographer, Gertrude had laboriously tinted and retouched his photographs. Although she had never studied dance or even seen a performance, as a child and a teenager, Gertrude would often go alone to the woods and dance for hours, imagining herself to be performing to large audiences. Like her son, Hugh Lynn, she also possessed very strong mental abilities. Her most influential previous lives included that of a beautiful dancer in Egypt, the adopted daughter of a Persian nomad and healer, the daughter of a Greek philosopher, and a member of the French court during the reigns of Louis XIV and Louis XV (538-5 and others).

Gladys Davis was told that one of her greatest strengths was her ability to take any obstacle and turn it into a "stepping-stone" toward personal development. She possessed great faith and was told that her innate desire was to provide "much good to many peoples" (288-1). She had been the daughter of a high priest in Egypt, the wife and "helpmeet" of a Persian nomad and leader, and a young mother in the French court who had given birth to an illegitimate child during the time of Louis XV (288-6 and others).

Edgar Cayce's own readings stated that he was prone to extremes. His main source of stability came from spirituality and his interest in spiritual development. As a soul, he was destined to give many individuals a new understanding and a personal experience with the helpfulness of psychic information. He would also provide individuals with much information regarding the healing arts. His most influential past lives included that of an Egyptian high priest, a Persian nomad and healer, a contemporary follower and missionary of Jesus, an illegitimate child during the reign of Louis XV, and an eighteenth-century American trapper and wanderer (294-8 and others).

According to the readings, two important periods for each of these four individuals included a lifetime in Egypt and one in the Holy Land during the time of Jesus. During the Egyptian experience all four had been physically incarnated. During the Holy Land experience, however, Edgar and Hugh Lynn were physically incarnated while Gladys and Gertrude acted as—what might be termed—"spirit guides" to their respective twin souls from the other side. According to the readings, Gladys acted as a guide to Edgar and Gertrude worked with Hugh Lynn.

In Persia, Gertrude had been the adopted daughter of a Persian healer and his wife, who would incarnate this time as Edgar Cayce and Gladys Davis. That lifetime would carry an interesting influence of role reversal when Gladys eventually moved into the Cayce home after her hire, becoming Edgar and Gertrude's "adopted daughter" in the present. In the Persian experience, Gladys Davis and Edgar Cayce had come together as twin souls with the purpose of creating a center of healing, education, and spiritual understanding—a work similar to that of A.R.E in the twentieth century.

In France, Edgar had lived a short time as the illegitimate son of Gladys but was apparently assassinated as a child because of a potential claim to the throne. That same role of parent and child had been repeated in Egypt when Gladys had been the daughter of Edgar and Gertrude. According to the readings, in terms of all these connections the greatest influence among each of the four was their shared lifetime in Egypt.

During the Egyptian experience, Edgar Cayce had been a high priest who had given the people a new understanding of many spiritual and universal truths. At that same time, Hugh Lynn had been the ruler and was charged with bringing the various peoples of his country together. The two shared a love for a beautiful dancer who worked in one of the temples—that dancer was Gertrude Cayce in the present. In time, Gertrude and Edgar came together and conceived a child, Gladys Davis. In large part because of his own jealousy, Hugh Lynn banished the high priest and the dancer from the country. He kept the child for himself as a means of clinging to a love that he had lost.

Understandably, all these various past-life relationships created a number of present-day influences among the four. As he was growing up, Hugh Lynn had to work with a jealousy and antagonism he felt toward his father. However, because of their joint Palestine experience, the two shared a deep love and respect for the work of Jesus. Gladys was occasionally torn between a brotherly love and a feeling of antagonism toward Hugh Lynn. Gertrude was easier on Hugh Lynn than was Edgar. Edgar and Gertrude often felt parental toward Gladys.

Obviously soul mate relationships consist of many past-life influences and urges that must be dealt with in the present. For that reason, the Cayce readings frequently reminded individuals that " . . . the real birthright of an individual entity is the will. No urge, then, no circumstance, no condition surpasses the will of an entity" (2272-1). Although past lives can influence the present in terms of subconscious memory, each individual retains freedom of choice in terms of how he or she chooses to deal with that memory. As a wonderful example, although Hugh Lynn had been ultimately responsible for banishing Edgar Cayce from Egypt and putting a stop to much of the high priest's work, in the present Hugh Lynn spent a lifetime making certain that his father's work survived.

As far as the present-day twin soul connection between Gladys Davis and Edgar Cayce, and Gertrude
Cayce and her son, Hugh Lynn, each of the individuals
was reminded that he or she had been brought together
for a "*oneness* of purpose." In terms of the relationship
between Gladys and Edgar, a reading reminded them:

Let then this, my children, be that lesson unto
you: In *oneness* of purpose, in oneness of spirit, in
oneness of mind, towards each and every one that
the bodies contact—for the entities, in their final
analysis, are one—and the intents toward each and
every individual should be to bring forward that
best element in each, that the lessons of the oneness of force may be made the better manifest in
the world. 288-19

Verifying the ongoing nature of a twin soul relationship, another reading stated that the two had been working together since "the morning stars sang together, and
the whispering winds brought the news of the coming of
man's indwelling" (294-8).
Likewise, Gertrude and Hugh Lynn were told:

Thus we find the emotions in which there arises
very close associations, as has been indicated from
the Egyptian sojourn also; not always as just son
and mother, but closer associations in a realm of
knowledge, or a realm of understanding, or realm
of indifference—for these are one when they are
turned in the same direction—as ye understand.
538-59

Throughout his life, Edgar Cayce provided individuals with accurate and helpful intuitive information. That
information has given countless individuals a new un-

derstanding of themselves as well as enable them to take a cocreative role in their enfolding life's process. Obviously, one of his purposes was the *information* itself. Along those same lines, one of Gladys Davis's purposes was to accurately record and keep track of the same information. Before Gladys Davis was hired as Cayce's secretary, the readings were not always recorded nor were they necessarily archived for the future. Although Cayce gave readings from 1901-1944, almost 95 percent of the readings on file at the Edgar Cayce Foundation are those which were recorded by Gladys after she was hired in 1923.

Gertrude Cayce, in addition to supporting her husband's work and being a source of balance in his life, acted as conductor for the readings. Her role was one that provided a stabilizing influence to the readings' process as well as to her family. In the same manner, Hugh Lynn Cayce became the stabilizing influence in the growth of his father's organization.

When Edgar Cayce died in January 1945, there were approximately 300 active members of the A.R.E. At the same time, the only book in print was Tom Sugrue's *There Is a River*, which had come about—in large part—because of Hugh Lynn's commitment to the idea. In May 1944, when the A.R.E. was simply a fledgling group of supporters very much committed to Edgar Cayce personally, Hugh Lynn outlined a visionary look at the future of the organization. Written while he was still serving overseas during World War II, his objectives for the Association included many seemingly unrealistic goals. Those goals included: a comprehensive magazine; ongoing lecture and conference programs; nationwide discussion groups; books on every phase of the Cayce information; one of the finest libraries in the world; a thorough indexing of the Cayce material by subject matter; and the ability to provide individuals with practical help from the readings.

When Hugh Lynn Cayce died in July 1982, his objectives for the organization had been realized. By that time, A.R.E. had greatly expanded its headquarters, become international in scope, grown to tens of thousands of members around the world, and was making available literally hundreds of books and other materials about his father's life and work. Although it is rarely discussed, Hugh Lynn often stressed the important role his mother played in his own upbringing and in his father's life of service to others. During the year of her death while he was still overseas and his mother was ill, Hugh Lynn expressed his feelings to her in a letter:

It is important for you to realize how much fun it has been being your son. So many times I have seen you faced with problems, conditions that I have known to crumple up so many people, and you have risen above them—and (the important thing) carried others with you. These things Edgar Evans [Hugh Lynn's younger brother] and I will not forget. To few people has there been entrusted the guidance of so many lives—not in the outward way to be seen by men, but in the background where the going was tough. These things I know, and will not forget. Never have I known of such unselfish love for two human beings as you have always shown toward Edgar Evans and me. This, too, I will never forget. It would be easy to go on and on.

It makes me proud to think of you. It makes me deeply happy to know how ready you are to pass through that other door. There is so much beauty in your living, my dear, that I cannot be sad at the possibility of you joining Dad. You held up his right hand, sometimes both hands here, so it does not surprise me that he may need you now.

We have come, Mother, to an understanding of

karma in a way that we have for a long time been
explaining to others, and I find that your life repre-
sents so much that is fine and beautiful that I cannot allow my selfish desires to mar this period of
waiting and wondering.

My prayers are that you will not suffer, my dear. I
know that you must realize how much love has
been, is, and always will be, yours.

Hugh Lynn
Case 538-9 Report File

Gertrude died on April 1, 1945, at seven o'clock on
Sunday, Easter morning, before seeing the letter which
had been written two days earlier on March 30. Gladys
Davis died in February 1986; she was the last of the four
to leave behind the work that had become the major focus of each of their lives. Inevitably, the relationships
among each of them, whether soul mates or twin souls,
will continue into the future. Their souls will draw them
together continuously with the goal of assisting one another spiritually and in the hopes of achieving whatever
work might be possible for the future.

# 8

## The Nature of Loneliness

My life as I have lived it had often seemed to me like a
story that has no beginning and no end. I had the feeling
that I was a historical fragment, an excerpt for which the
preceding and succeeding text was missing . . . I could
well imagine that I might have lived in former centuries
and there encountered questions I was not yet able to
answer; that I had to be born again because I had not
fulfilled the task that was given to me. When I die, my
deeds will follow along with me—that is how I imagine
it. I will bring with me what I have done. In the meantime it is important to insure that I do not stand at the
end with empty hands . . .

Carl Jung
*Memories, Dreams, Reflections*

One of the most surprising things about the readings
given for people who were lonely and were looking
for friends, companionship, or a marriage partner is that
Cayce never told them where to find a relationship. Instead, the focus of the information was that there was

something individuals were supposed to be doing with their time alone. Oftentimes, the readings saw loneliness as a period needing to encompass both personal growth and healing as well as a time of reaching out to others who were less fortunate. Individuals who were suffering from all kinds of loneliness were frequently told to begin discovering their unique soul talents and abilities and to find ways in which they could be helpful to others. Cayce believed that once individuals put their efforts in these directions, relationships would inevitably be drawn to them.

For example, a twenty-nine-year-old divorced woman was concerned about when she would marry again and wondered whether she had met her husband-to-be. Cayce told her to take her focus off getting married and instead to become more concerned about her physical and mental health and what she was accomplishing within herself: "Accomplishing something in self *first!* Gain an understanding of self's relationships, of self's relationship to the divine as may be manifested—and *find* an *ideal!*" (5615-1).

In another instance, a thirty-nine-year-old widow obtained a reading in which she wanted to know whether or not the opportunity to marry again would ever present itself. Her husband had died of alcoholism, and she was lonely and looking for direction. Understandably, she had been focusing on her own needs, trying to make herself less lonely and to become happier in the process. Cayce told her that—when the time felt right—she needed to change her approach:

Do something for someone else! Make their lives happy, make their lives worth while, and then there may be those experiences that will come! But arise to that consciousness that if ye would have life, if ye would have friends, if ye would have love, these

things ye must expend. For only that ye give away
do ye possess. 1786-2

In 1930 a forty-eight-year-old woman, who was also a
widow, wrote Edgar Cayce seeking help. Her letter stated,
in part:

> I have been a widow for fifteen years—and while
> my time is fully occupied I am a very lonely soul—
> craving for companionship. There have been many
> men in my life, but somehow never THE right one
> for whom I cared enough to marry. Can you tell me
> if I am ever to be married again? This is the subject
> for which I need your help. Will you do that for me?
> I trust I may hear from you and tell me when I can
> expect a reading . . . Case 1740-1 Report File

During the course of her reading, Cayce told the
woman that her loneliness was caused by several conditions. In spite of the fact that she was "well balanced,
physically attractive, [and] mentally *superb*" she was also
quick tempered and often regretted the way she spoke
to others. She possessed talents and abilities that desired
to be expressed and continued to pull at her from within.
On a number of occasions she had blamed others for her
experiences in life. The reading suggested that she
needed to take the responsibility for turning her life's direction to more constructive channels. She was encouraged to use her abilities in a positive direction, to focus
on her ideals, and to keep physically fit. As she followed
these suggestions, all that she needed in life would be
drawn to her, including the mate that she sought.

For a twenty-four-year-old woman who asked Cayce
in 1939, "Where is the man whom I should marry? and
how may I meet him?" she was told, "This should be the
natural consequence of associations in thy social and

everyday life. When thou hast fully prepared thy body, thy mind, for fulfilling the duties of home building, he *will* appear" (951-4). A forty-six-year-old man who sought companionship was reminded that he still needed to work on himself. He was told to ponder the question, "If ye can't live very well with yourself—can ye with others?" (5392-1).

A sixty-eight-year-old professor, who complained that he lacked meaningful friendship and companionship, asked how he could remedy the situation. For too long he felt he had lived an isolated existence. Cayce advised him, "So give out of self to *attract* to thee those who need what thou hast to give" (3056-1). On another occasion, a forty-five-year-old woman who wanted to know "the best outlets for my loneliness" was advised: "Be busy in keeping optimistic and in helping somebody who is in a worse fix than yourself—and there are millions of 'em!" (1540-6).

Although her primary desire was to have a husband and a family, a twenty-six-year-old woman was reminded that there were many other areas she could pursue in the present. A reading told her that she had talents as a writer, as a teacher, as a secretary, as a motivator, even as a minister. She was encouraged to choose some field in which to become active until the opportunity for marriage presented itself. Cayce suggested, "Apply this as given in the present, and His blessings and His grace and His mercy and His love will keep thee from that fear of loneliness, from that of despondency; bringing joy and a joyousness in a service to thy fellow man" (945-1).

A forty-five-year-old woman, whose family had died during the war and who had no living relatives except for a sixteen-year-old daughter, was afraid that she would become totally devastated when the time came for her child to leave home. In 1944 she wrote Edgar

Cayce asking him to tell her about the fears she had regarding being alone:

> All this seems to lead to one thing: I am very
> lonely, and am desperate when I think that in a
> couple more years I won't even have my daughter
> to make a home for, guide, and love. What is wrong
> with me? I get a lot of compliments on being attrac-
> tive, and even charming; but socially I am such a
> failure. Of course, I am not young, and it is only the
> young who have variety of partners from [the] op-
> posite sex to choose from; men I know are all mar-
> ried; any men who were interested in me always
> had dishonorable intentions; I seem to be out of step
> with the times—lots of drinking and loose morals.
> But deep within me I feel that I am doing right; that
> I could not be otherwise, for then I would lose my
> own self-respect, and just won't pay such high price
> for popularity. Am I to live the rest of my life alone,
> lonely, and miserable, happiness passing me by? Is
> there any ray of hope? Case 5728-1 Report File

Cayce told the woman that she had much to share
with others. She was encouraged to begin by using a talent she possessed, which was her ability to help people
set aside the cares of their daily lives. The reading encouraged her to start bringing small groups of people
together, either as a means of everyone in the group
sharing their talents with one another or as small groups
to which the woman herself could begin teaching meta-
physical classes. Cayce stated that she was a natural en-
tertainer and a wonderful conversationalist. She also
possessed a mystical air and knew a great deal about the
mysteries of the unknown. Her talent with entertain-
ment and the ability to inspire others came from a lifetime in Greece. In the Holy Land, she had been a Hittite

deeply involved in the studies of the mysteries of life. When she asked, "How can I fill the great gap in my life?" he replied, "Read what has been indicated, and commence that which the entity can supply that is much needed in the lives of individuals, in either direction."

One young woman was told that she often experienced periods of doubt, fear, and loneliness because she had so frequently repressed her desire for self-expression. She was encouraged to stop thwarting herself, to realize that the only individual holding her back was herself, and to begin expressing her talents (1968-5). Although it would be ten years before she married and had two children, by her own account she was very happy and grateful that she had waited to find the right spouse. She once wrote Gladys Davis, "We believe that waiting until later in life to find each other has made us appreciate our marriage even more than if it had come when we were much younger."

The Cayce readings saw loneliness as a prompting from the subconscious mind to turn within in the case of a fifty-four-year-old housewife. By her own admission, the woman often felt lonely and misunderstood by those around her. She was told that she had a talent for writing, especially in stories or books for teenage girls. From Cayce's perspective, the woman's loneliness would lessen to the same degree she accessed the talents and abilities she possessed at a soul level but had not yet utilized (2992-1).

In the same manner, another woman was told that her loneliness was partially due to the fact that she frequently suppressed her ego and abilities. That suppression had also created a physical imbalance in her body which was making the depression worse, causing her to feel "far away, lonely, that nobody particularly cares, and that self does not care particularly" (3102-1). In addition to recommendations for the physical problem and encouragement for her to find physical and mental balance in her life, Cayce reminded the woman that "mind was the builder" and the thoughts she was thinking were having an ongoing effect upon her mental-physical condition.

In May 1944 a woman wrote Cayce: "I am alone in the world, fifty-five, and growing old alone, when I desperately need family life, love, and companionship . . . I carry a smiling face to the world and am soloist in a choir, singing inspirationally always, but in my heart I am a little child, alone . . . " (Case 5124-1 Report File). The woman was told in her reading that she had too frequently suppressed her own talents, desires, and inclinations because of the opinion of others. This repression had been so extreme that she had stunted her personal growth. If she was to begin working with those things that she knew to do and to pursue her life's interests, she would meet a marriage companion. If she continued to suppress her feelings and the activities with which she wanted to become involved, she was destined to remain single.

In another instance, a thirty-seven-year-old housewife was told that her sense of loneliness was due in part to feeling unappreciated and not fully understood "even by those closest to the entity." She was encouraged to begin working with spiritual ideals and to cultivate faith in herself which would also enable her to begin to feel more comfortable expressing herself (2170-1).

A fifty-year-old woman found herself experiencing loneliness because her children had grown and left home. One of her reasons for obtaining a reading was to inquire whether she and her husband should move into a smaller house. Cayce told her that a change of locations might do her well, but in order to overcome her loneliness, she primarily needed to find ways in which she could be of assistance to others. In addition to keeping in touch with her loved ones, she was encouraged to discover ways she could be of assistance to those with whom she was already familiar (79-1).

A forty-two-year-old artist was told that she had subconsciously delayed marriage because, in many of her previous incarnations, marriage with the wrong partner had "brought confusion." She was encouraged to continue her artistic work with children and, in time, the appropriate relationship would present itself. As to what she should do in the meantime when she felt lonely, she was reminded that ultimately she was never alone:

> Yet, remember—and in the analyzing of self and of self's problems—the lesson that is to be learned here and now. And know that thou art *never* alone if ye hold to that purpose that ye may be at one with Him. For His promise has been, "I will not leave thee—I will be with thee always." And again may ye, in seeking—oft—oft—hear that voice within, "Be not afraid, it is I." 2397-1

A woman who wanted to know why she often felt so lonely and why she had so few friends was told that in actuality she had many friends, but that she had not cultivated true friendship with any of them. Rather than simply seeing them socially or in day-to-day life, Cayce encouraged her to begin showing them the same love that she was seeking. There were many that were not as fortunate as she was and she could be of great aid and assistance to them. In return, she would find the love that she sought (2401-1).

A man who stated that one of his problems was being too self-conscious was advised to "Lose self in doing something for someone else!" in order to overcome the problem (5420-1). When he wanted to know how he could find the right girl to marry, his reading told him: "Act, live, in that way and manner as is befitting one *de-*

*serving* the kind, the ideal—and it will *come* to pass."

A thirty-six-year-old woman, who felt lonely and apathetic about life, obtained a reading. Not satisfied with her line of work, she wanted to know if there was any way she could find "some semblance of a contented, useful, and even happy life . . . " and whether she could "hope for love and marriage, [and] a family of my own?" Cayce told her that she was a very pleasant person in spite of the fact that she often had the tendency to become overwrought over "very trifling experiences." She possessed abilities in the creative arts, in writing, in acting, even on the radio. Her past lives had frequently involved entertaining others as well as activities when she had worked with children.

For the most part, her life was not utilizing her creativity. Cayce advised her to seek employment in a creative channel that would allow her to better express herself. The reading assured her that when she became involved in a more suitable occupation, a companion would be drawn to her. When she asked about her proper course of action, Cayce replied:

> Just keep trying in the attitude of asking daily that the entity be guided in doing and choosing that which is the greater benefit, not for the entity alone, but the contribution to making the world a better place for others to live in. 5248-1

In addition to loneliness being a time for personal reflection, growth, and reaching out to others, the readings told some individuals that they were unconsciously creating their own isolation by their responses and reactions to others. For example, in 1936 a forty-nine-year-old man involved in the shoe business obtained a physical reading for circulation problems (1238-3). After Cayce provided him with the information, the man asked: "What is there in my make-up that keeps people from an enduring friendship with me?" He was told that he possessed a critical mind and the talents of a counselor. As a result, people were often drawn to him. However, when they asked for his opinion, he was too critical in providing "his assessments." Cayce reminded him that whenever people came to him for help, it was not an opportunity for him to feel gratified about how much he knew; rather, the focus needed to be on truly attempting to be of help to others.

A fifty-one-year-old artist who frequently felt unappreciated was encouraged to begin cultivating her appreciation of others. Cayce told her that whatever she put out would eventually come back to her. Reminded of the spiritual basis of life, she was also encouraged to begin using the following prayer:

> LORD, LET ME FILL THAT PLACE IN THE LIVES OF OTHERS AS THOU HAST GIVEN AND DO GIVE THE OPPORTUNITY, IN SUCH MEASURES AND SUCH MANNERS THAT OTHERS MAY COME TO KNOW THAT LIFE IS OF THEE, IN THEE. 1823-1

Edgar Cayce frequently discussed the dynamics of a universal law that he called "like attracts like." Simply stated, individuals are constantly attracting to themselves the same things they are putting out. Rather than experiencing the negative aspects of this law, Cayce encouraged individuals to become more conscious of how they were treating others and to begin giving to others the very same things they would like to receive in return:

> And if ye would find that which is harmony, created in thy experience, then create same for others. If ye would know friendships, show self to be friendly. If ye would be in those experiences of hav-

ing others think well or speak well of thee, be lovely then to all. For in the manner ye treat the least of thy associates or thy fellow man, so ye do unto the best or to the God that is within thee. 2023-1

Parents of an eleven-year-old girl were told that their daughter would find great companionship with herself, which was a true gift, but at the same time they needed to encourage her to be a good companion to others. The girl was inclined to be too critical—a trait that, if not corrected, would lead her to loneliness later in life. The reading advised the parents to teach her a valuable lesson: "To minimize faults in others as ye would have others minimize thine own faults or shortcomings" (2648-1).

Another young woman was told that her tendency to belittle herself and her abilities was causing a great deal of loneliness. She was encouraged to recapture the spiritual faith she had once had during a lifetime in Rome. By focusing on her personal spirituality and beliefs, she would gain self-confidence and overcome her loneliness (2803-2).

A thirty-year-old pilot was told that his loneliness was frequently caused by the fact that he was hesitant to give his love to others. He was encouraged to be especially aware of how he treated others when he himself was lonely or in turmoil. Cayce also reminded him that all that he put out emotionally would come back to him:

If ye would have friends be friendly. If ye would have love, love others. If ye would have hope manifest same in thy dealings with others. Though there may be periods when hope seems abandoned, when oppression seems to be on self, look not upon same for condemnations. For, as ye are forgiving, so are ye forgiven; as ye hope, as ye work, as ye manifest, this, that or the other characteristic, it

brings its reward—if done in the spirit of truth.
3184-1

From her Cayce reading, a bookkeeper learned that
the cause of her loneliness was due to her quick mind
and sarcastic nature. Apparently she so feared having
others be critical of her that, in an effort to shield herself
from criticism, she was often sarcastic to those around
her. Cayce told her that she needed to redirect her mental abilities so that she could cultivate and apply a new
outlook on life (5098-1). With persistency and consis-
tency, she could change the way she was responding to
people, they would change the way they were responding to her, and she would no longer have to worry about
loneliness.

On several occasions, the root of someone's loneliness
was traced to experiences in a past lifetime. In one instance a government employee, who often felt lonely
when she was with other people and even when she was
in a crowded room, was told that some of her feelings
were traceable to a past life at the time of the Crusades
(1183-1). Apparently, at that time, in order to take care of
the "upkeep of the home," she had frequently been left
behind while her family went elsewhere. The readings
suggested that when she felt the same loneliness in the
present, she needed to consider it an internal prompting for self-reflection and the opportunity to begin seeking her own inner self.

A thirty-four-year-old woman was told that her loneliness was due to the fact that she frequently separated
herself emotionally from others. As a result, she was often lonely within herself and "the more lonely, the more
people there are about the entity." A reading traced her
hesitancy to open up emotionally to a past-life experience when she had suffered a broken heart and had
sworn to herself that she "would never again in material

experiences love those that could disappoint and bring experiences that would cause the heartache in the flesh" (1747-3). She was encouraged to show more affection toward others and to begin cultivating friendships with those around her. By so doing, she would not only have her own needs for love met, but she would also be helping those who needed her love.

A thirty-one-year-old divorcée was told that she so feared being alone that rather than being by herself, she often associated "with those who are not altogether to the liking of the entity." Once married to a "completely immoral and irresponsible" minister, her fear of being alone was not solely because of her failed marriage. A reading pointed out that in her most recent past life she had been among a group of explorers and had inadvertently been left behind when the others returned to their native country. Her fears could be overcome by working with herself and turning within (958-3).

A fifty-three-year-old man loved people and loved being around people, but he felt that people withdrew from him whenever he approached them. Even in a crowd he was often lonely and withdrew from others because he felt that they were withdrawing from him. Cayce told him that this situation had begun when he was a Saxon. At the time, he loved having people look up to him: "There the entity was looked up to by his fellow men— and he liked it! Yet instead of using it to be of greater service, you liked it too well and others forgot you" (3544-1).

Regardless of whether loneliness was traceable to a past life, one's upbringing, or even a physical-emotional condition, the Cayce readings took the same approach in solving the situation. For example, a forty-seven-year-old woman was told that her feelings of loneliness and depression were due, in part, to a chemical problem caused by her digestion. In addition to providing her the names of medication which would help her digestive problem, Cayce also reminded her of the powerful capacity she possessed within her own mind. She was encouraged to facilitate an awareness of her connection and "at-onement" with the rest of Creation. Those things taken together would bring "the better physical as well as mental attitude in the reflections through the body" (1100-34).

When a chiropractor, who was experiencing difficulty in his relationship with his wife, asked to what extent his childhood had incapacitated him for "a normal, happy marriage," Cayce replied:

Just as much as the individual entity lets it have. For when ye were a child, ye thought as a child, but when ye became a man ye should have put away childish things and not blamed others for same. For each soul is an entity, body, mind, soul. If it will use its will, in applying the fruits of the spirit to those conditions about it, the entity may attune itself to the infinite. If it attempts to abuse such, the entity pays the price. Just as ye may see about thee. As a tree grows you may bear it and use it and grind it in the shape desired. So may an individual entity, as it is trained, grow. It has those complexes but it also has its own individuality . . . 4083-1

The chiropractor continued his line of questioning by asking, "Have any adolescent experiences incapacitated the entity for a normal, happy marriage?" The response came, "Read what has been given. All of thy problems are here within self." When he asked, "Psychoanalytically speaking, what is the entity's emotional age?" the reply was short: "About two months."

Parents of a young boy were told that their son had the tendency to experience periods of loneliness in his life. When those occasions arose, Cayce recommended that he get in touch with music that would touch his soul and help him work through those periods of loneliness (3203-1).

When people were looking for a mate, the readings often asked them to do some personal reflection as to what they were looking for. If they were looking for someone to satisfy an emotional or a physical desire, then they would not be happy in marriage. Instead, the best motive for marriage was to find someone they could be helpful to and by whom they could be helped in return. From Cayce's perspective, true love was not simply an emotion, but the act of losing oneself in service to another. True love also embodied the bringing together of complements that were not identical but would instead enable each individual to experience a "more helpful, more sustaining, more . . . well-*rounded* life . . . " (364-7).

When a twenty-year-old girl wanted to know in what line of work her future husband would be employed, a reading told her: "Whether he's a street sweeper or the president you'll know him! It isn't the line of work you choose, it's as heart answers to heart and body to body" (308-13).

To a thirty-eight-year-old man who asked if marriage was advisable, Cayce replied: "It's advisable at any time if you find the right person!" When he asked, "Have I as yet met the girl whom I will eventually marry?" the reply was, "This depends upon self. You've met several that you *could* marry, but *would* you!" When he asked to reveal her name, Cayce told him that it was a choice he had to make within himself. Within ten months he was married (622-7).

In a final example, in 1943 a thirty-seven-year-old woman left a job she loved in order to find a husband. A friend had also advised the woman that her career, which was taking care of children in their home, was not "using the varied talents entrusted to her by a kind Creator." In May of that year, she obtained a reading and inquired whether or not she was destined to remain single or if there was a chance that she might get married. She also wanted to know whether it was best to leave her home in New York.

The reading told her that "within the next three years" she would have an opportunity for great joy if she instead focused on her purpose in life, which was not simply to be thought of as a nursemaid to children. Instead, she was told to realize her importance as "a teacher, as a companion, as an instructress, as one that may guide not only the body-spiritual but the body-mental and the body-physical of the young . . . " (2988-2). She was also advised that it would be best for her to remain in New York. After the reading, even though the woman's loneliness had not been solved, she felt relieved that she did not have to focus on finding a husband but instead could return to her work with children.

One month later, the woman accidentally ran into her former employer at a department store. The family had not been able to find anyone to replace her, so they pleaded with her to "please come back with us." She wrote Edgar and Gertrude Cayce to tell them of her new attitude: "So thus I am back in my old place—which I left four weeks ago today—returned a new person with a joyful outlook on things and my work."

Although nothing was heard from the woman for a number of years, in 1958 she wrote Gladys Davis a letter, which included a follow-up report:

Dear Gladys.
. . . it warmed my heart to see you had been "searching" for me—but I have never left N.Y. state—how could I? The Cayce reading said—I would find my "Husband"—in and around New

York—and according to the reading it ought to have
been around 1946—and not 1948 when we did
meet—But as usual the reading WAS right—it was
us; in time—when we got talking about the Cayce
reading we found out—that we had BOTH turned
down a position which would have brought us together in 1946—see—well—so here I am—Mrs.
[2988] . . . Case 2988-5 Report File

Cayce had done it again.

# 9

## *Conception and Soul Attraction*

For the average man or woman, however, to become parents is to open a channel for a soul that will enhance their lives or make them miserable depending upon their attitudes at the moment of that channel's creation. It is a frightening prospect and those who know nothing of Kabbalah or who dismiss reincarnation gamble with their very lives in the act of procreation.

> Rabbi Philip S. Berg, Ph.D., Director
> Research Centre of Kabbalah International

Edgar Cayce frequently told individuals that one of the most important services they could perform was to agree to become parents for a soul coming into the earth. Many individuals were also advised that one of their soul's purposes was to create an environment for home, family, and the raising of children. Cayce once stated, "For no greater office is there for an entity to fill than to be a channel through which a soul may find the way of experience into the material plane" (480-30).

Not only did the readings confirm the important responsibility entrusted to parents in the raising of children, but Cayce also believed that parents were actually accountable for attracting the specific children to whom they gave birth. To be sure, soul attraction was dependent upon causative factors such as previous soul experiences between parent and child and the potential environment and upbringing the parents could provide in the present. However, the readings stated that the parents' ideals and purposes at the moment of conception as well as throughout the entire period of gestation had a great deal to do with the soul who would ultimately decide to be born into a specific family. For that reason, Cayce told expectant parents that with the proper preparation and attitude, they had the opportunity to become channels for a soul who could bring light, love, and hope into the earth.

According to the readings, the thoughts, the feelings, and the activities of expectant parents create a type of vibration or energy field which make it possible only for certain souls to come into the earth through them. Essentially parents provide a physical channel through which a soul can manifest; however, that channel has to be "in tune" with the spiritual development (and resulting needs and lessons) of the incoming soul. When Cayce was giving readings, parents, especially expectant mothers, were constantly advised to maintain a cheerful, hopeful, spiritual outlook, to fill their minds with uplifting materials, thoughts, and activities, and to make certain they didn't neglect their own spiritual life throughout the entire pregnancy.

The influence parents have in the process of soul attraction was clearly explained to a twenty-four-year-old expectant mother who asked a series of questions about her pregnancy and her unborn child. When she inquired, "What mental attitude should I keep always before me during the coming months?" the response was:

Depends upon what character of individual entity is desired. More beauty, music—if that is desired to be a part of the entity; art, and the like. Or is it to be purely mechanical? If purely mechanical, then think about mechanics—work with those things. And don't think that they won't have their effect, as the impressions give that opportunity.

Here is something that each and every mother should know. The manner in which the attitude is kept has much to do with the character of the soul that would choose to enter through those channels at the particular period. This has been indicated as the attitude, "If ye love me and keep my commandments, I will love you—as ye do unto others, ye do unto me—." Does this seem strange, or isn't it consistent with God's plan of creation? That attitude held, then, during these periods, presents the opportunity for the type or character of soul seeking expression. 2803-6

When she asked, "Would my working outside the home now be injurious to the child?" Cayce reminded her of the important role she played during the "formative period" of her pregnancy:

Hence it depends upon what character of individual you hope to have! One that will be a workaday, material-minded, one looking for the making of money, the making of position, the making of this or that? Not that this would necessarily be the outward attitude, but the real innate attitude deep within the soul of the entity attracted.

In another instance, a thirty-four-year-old expectant

mother was told that the attitudes she and her husband
held during her pregnancy would be the determining
factor in deciding the nature, attitude, and character of
the child they brought into the earth (457-10). For that
reason, Cayce recommended that she read certain biblical passages during her pregnancy and suggested
Deuteronomy 30, the fourteenth through seventeenth
chapters of John, and the story of Hannah contained in
the Book of Samuel. When she asked, "Is not the mother
when carrying a child very close to God?" the reading
replied, "If she puts herself so! If not, it is merely a physical condition." At the end of her reading, Cayce reminded the woman that the soul which would come to
them was a child of God and that, as parents, she and
her husband were simply being entrusted with its care
and development, "for, remember, the soul that is
brought into the earth is only lent to thee by the Lord.
And the impressions, and that purpose that ye build into
that, is that ye send back to thy Maker in the end."

A twenty-three-year-old expectant mother who wanted
to know the best attitude to keep in mind during her
pregnancy was advised: "Keep happy, and keep that expectancy of that character and disposition that is desired in the offspring; knowing and realizing in self—as
should be in the companionship—that this is being a
channel for the manifestation of God's love in the earth.
Not as a duty or obligation, but as the opportunity for
being a handmaid of the Lord" (2635-2).

In 1935, confirmation was given a young couple that
they had conceived a child. They were advised to become mindful of the attitudes they held and the activities with which they were involved, as well as the
associations and friendships they cultivated during the
pregnancy. Since they ultimately would be responsible
for the soul they brought into the earth, Cayce suggested
that they hold in mind the desire that their child could

become a channel of hope and blessings to others (934-3). Another couple was told that—provided they kept the proper attitude—it would be possible for the soul that would be attracted to them as channels to manifest God's love in the earth (575-1).

After the birth of her son, one woman was told that she and her husband had attracted a very exceptional child because of the wonderful attitude they had held in mind during her pregnancy. Their child's soul history included some important past-life experiences and the boy possessed rare musical talent. The parents were assured their son was destined to become a great musician, provided he was given appropriate upbringing and direction (4098-1).

Although the attitudes of mother and father are extremely important during pregnancy, Cayce made it clear that the entire family, as well, could have an effect upon the selection of the incoming soul. In one instance, a woman and her husband moved in with the woman's aunt during her pregnancy. After the child's birth, Cayce told the family that the move had been a purposeful experience and had occurred because of a past-life relationship between all four of them in ancient Persia. When the aunt asked how such experiences occurred, Cayce stated, "For each soul, each entity, *constantly* meets self. And if each soul would but understand, those hardships which are accredited much to others are caused most by self. *Know* that in those you are meeting *thyself!*" (845-4).

Oftentimes, individuals were told that they needed to provide their children with the appropriate attitudes and direction not only during conception and childhood, but throughout the formative teenage years. Parents were frequently reminded of the important role that spirituality needed to play throughout the course of their child's development. Because of the dynamics of free will, even a soul with great potential could fail in a particular lifetime if she or he were not given appropriate spiritual direction.

On one occasion, parents of an eleven-year-old boy were told that as long as they gave their son the spiritual foundation his soul craved, "*Great* may be the accomplishments of this entity during this experience" (1700-1). However, if those spiritual principles were not cultivated especially during the next few years, their son would become especially material-minded, selfish, and would eventually bring "many a sorrow" into their lives.

During the wife's pregnancy, another couple wanted to know if there was anything they could do that would help their child's development both physically and mentally. They were told to seek "perfect cooperation" with each other and to hold in mind the proper attitudes physically, mentally, morally, and spiritually. Those attitudes would be responsible for the soul they attracted as well as its potentials for development (903-8). On a number of occasions, Edgar Cayce used stories from the Bible to illustrate the important role parents played in pregnancy and soul attraction, including the story of Hannah and the story of Isaac and Rebekah.

The story of Hannah is told in the Book of Samuel. Barren and desperately desiring a child, Hannah prayed fervently for a son. She promised that if she were given a son, she would "give him unto the Lord all the days of his life." Shortly thereafter, her trust was rewarded and she became pregnant. Throughout her pregnancy, she apparently kept in mind an attitude of spiritual expectancy, and when her son was born, she named him Samuel. Remembering her promise, Hannah consecrated her child's life in service to God, and Samuel grew to become the first of the Hebrew prophets and a ruler of his country. Edgar Cayce felt that the story of Hannah was important because she lived at a time when the earth needed "great spiritual awakening" (5037-2)—a time, Cayce believed, which was similar to our own. Because of Hannah's dedication and faith, she had been able to bring a great soul into the earth who grew to become of much service to humankind.

From the readings' perspective, the story of Isaac and Rebekah presents an interesting portrayal of two parents having very different ideals and attitudes about the child they desired. According to Cayce, those differing desires began at conception and lasted throughout the entire pregnancy, resulting in the outcome being that "*Both* attitudes found expression." Rebekah gave birth to twin boys, Esau and Jacob, who were very different from one another. Esau, his father's favorite, grew to be "the hairy one" and loved the outdoors and the tracking of game. Jacob, his mother's favorite, was the quiet and gentle one who would grow to become the father and the spiritual leader of the nation of Israel. In discussing the brothers, Cayce stated:

> Though conceived at once, born together, they were far separated in their purposes, their aims, their hopes; one holding to that which made body, mind and soul coordinant; the other satisfying, gratifying the appetites of the physical and mental without coordinating same through its spiritual relationships . . .
>
> Do ye think that one received a different instruction from the other? Each received the same, yet their reaction, their choice of that in the environment made physical characteristics that varied in their activity. 281-48

Although Cayce was well aware of the fact that conception could be a wholly carnal activity, he stated that there was a much greater possibility. Since the attitudes and ideals held by the channels who would become parents had an effect from the moment of conception onward, it was best to become cognizant of the possibility of being used as a channel to bring God's love and spirit into the earth. Without spiritual ideals or higher attitudes, parents could just as likely become the channels for a soul who desired to manifest chaos or even disorder and destruction.

The fact that several souls may be deciding whether or not to choose specific individuals as parents is illustrated in the contemporary experience of a woman named Thelma. Thelma and her husband were in their late thirties and had two children. After the birth of their youngest child, for at least two years the couple had tried for a third pregnancy but without success. For that reason, Thelma began to think that maybe they weren't supposed to have any more children. Then she had a dream suggesting she was about to receive an "unexpected package."

In the dream she was sitting in her living room opening Christmas packages that had been sent to her—but even in the dream she knew it wasn't Christmas. At first she didn't think the dream had anything to do with having a baby. After all, she had not been able to get pregnant a third time. A short time later, she and her husband prayed and meditated together about the advisability of having another child. Immediately thereafter Thelma discovered she was pregnant. Because she knew about Cayce's emphasis on the importance of attitudes and what the mind dwelt upon during pregnancy, Thelma worked with spiritual principles, uplifting reading, meditation and prayer, and asked that the right soul be drawn to her and her husband.

During her pregnancy, Thelma had another dream that seemed to concern her brother. In real life, her brother had frequently been depressed—even to the point of wanting to commit suicide. In the dream, her brother asked her if she would allow him to come into the earth again through her if he killed himself. Thelma replied "no" and stated that she was already working with "five entities" who were considering her as a mother. As she spoke in her dream, she saw five figures— four men and a woman—standing near her, although she could not see their features or their faces. She knew that the figures were souls who were being drawn to the possibility of having her and her husband as parents. Months later, when Thelma gave birth to a little girl, she had no doubt that her child was one of the same souls she had seen in her dream.

Edgar Cayce frequently advised parents to watch their dreams during pregnancy. Not only could dreams provide practical information about the child, its sex, its delivery date, and any health-care measures that needed to be taken, but dreams could also help in the selection of a name as well as provide past-life information about their child's soul. In 1925 Cayce interpreted one woman's dream and told her that the dream indicated she was not physically prepared for pregnancy and needed to become so or to take the proper precautions. Not heeding his advice, she found herself pregnant a few weeks later and miscarried within the first trimester (136-22). Fourteen months later she successfully gave birth to a son.

In her book *Born to Live,* Gladys T. McGarey, M.D., details the insights that dreams can provide, along the same lines mentioned by Edgar Cayce, including health and past lives. A founding physician of the American Holistic Medical Association, Dr. McGarey has spent more than fifty years as a family physician and has experienced countless occasions when dreams provided accurate, insightful information. In just one example, a man dreamed that an individual in a white coat met him in the lobby of a hotel, handed him an object (which the man knew to be his wife's IUD), and stated, "Your wife is pregnant." Although the man discussed the dream with his wife, both thought it nonsense because she had been using an IUD for over six years without a problem. However, the dream turned out to be prophetic. The following spring, his wife's IUD was removed just moments before the birth of their child.

Because a soul can choose whether or not to be born into a certain situation right up until birth, the readings state that there is a difference between physical conception and the moment when the soul enters the body. Apparently, a soul can choose to be born into a body anytime from several hours before birth to even twenty-four hours after birth. There is also at least one reference to Sudden Infant Death Syndrome (SIDS) discussed in the readings even before the term existed. Cayce stated that the child had chosen to leave the earth a short time after her birth because the soul had come to the conclusion that the environment which would be provided by the parents would not be a helpful experience and had therefore decided "*not* to maintain the consciousness in materiality" (2390-2). The reading went on to state that this decision to leave the body was sometimes possible at a soul level even up until the age of three.

In 1940, when a thirty-seven-year-old housewife wanted to know if she had deliberately chosen her parents, she was told: "A whole dissertation might be given on this subject!" (2170-1). Cayce stated that essentially two laws had a tremendous influence upon souls coming into the earth. The laws are the law of cause and effect and the law of attraction. In part, the law of cause and effect deals with an individual's soul memory and the lessons, relationships, and experiences it had built in the past. The law of attraction acts as a sort of universal magnet that draws a soul to those experiences and conditions it needs for the soul lessons it desires to achieve. With these two laws in mind, the woman had been drawn to her parents because they had shared past-life experiences together, and she had also been attracted to them because of the environment they could provide for her in the present.

In a final example from the Cayce readings, a couple sought advice and guidance which would enable them to become the best channels for a soul desiring to incarnate into the earth (341-48). They were advised to cooperate with one another and to establish a mutual desire for bringing such a child into the earth. Cayce recommended that the ultimate desire was to enable God to fulfill His purposes with the two of them: "Thus the type soul will be given thee that is in keeping with thy abilities to contribute to mankind, to the world, the channel for a soul needed in the present." The attitude each was to hold in mind was: "Lord, use Thou me—my body, my mind, my purpose—as a channel of blessings to others."

The reading assured them that God knew their strengths and abilities and would send them a soul who could benefit from the upbringing they would provide. They were encouraged to work with prayer and meditation throughout the entire pregnancy, to continue to hold the proper ideals, and to maintain an ever-present attitude of hopeful expectancy. They were also to live purposefully, knowing that God would work with them if they would allow Him to. When the couple asked if it were advisable to desire a specific sex for their child, Cayce recommended that if they truly wished to cooperate with spirit, the best desire they could maintain was simply, *"Lord, have Thy ways with us."*

Almost exactly one year later, the couple became the proud parents of a baby boy. The readings would eventually confirm that the couple and their child had been together previously and that each was simply picking up a soul mate relationship from the past.

# 10

## *Creating Soul Mate Relationships*

I cannot think of permanent enmity between man and
man, and believing as I do in the theory of rebirth, I live
in the hope that if not in this birth, in some other birth, I
shall be able to hug all humanity in friendly embrace.

Mahatma Gandhi

For the first half of the twentieth century, individuals
from all walks of life and religious backgrounds came
to Edgar Cayce and received advice for improving their
relationships with spouses, friends, families, work associates, even enemies. Regardless of who the relationship
was with or for how many years (or lifetimes) the relationship had been difficult, Cayce outlined the same
principles that individuals could use for healing their
various relationships. From his perspective, creating
soul mate relationships with every individual in our life
is one of our purposes for being in the earth.

In terms of a very difficult relationship, perhaps questions that an individual might ask is "Why bother?" "Why

is it so important that we work on healing every one of our relationships?" Over the years, in seeking answers to these very questions, individuals have found a number of premises contained in the Edgar Cayce information:

- Ultimately, all relationships have the potential to be a purposeful and a helpful experience in terms of soul growth and personal transformation.
- We learn most about ourselves through our interactions with others.
- Our relationships with one another are destined to be repeated until they are healed.
- As souls seeking personal wholeness, our goal is to eventually create soul mate relationships with every individual in our lives.

For a moment, if we think about the one person in our lives whom we love most of all, we might ask ourselves, "What is the nature of that relationship?" If we imagine the feelings of unconditional love and acceptance we hold toward that individual, we might ponder, "What does that really feel like?" If we could create a sense of the devotion we have to this person in terms of wanting only the best for him or her and our willingness to be of service in that regard, we might examine, "What kind of love places the needs of others above our own?" If we can only get a sense of the nature and dynamics of this type of a relationship, this is exactly how we will eventually feel about every single soul. The Edgar Cayce readings suggest that until every individual has truly learned to love in this manner, her or his soul growth is not finished.

Rather than becoming depressed by the enormity of such a personal goal, the readings also contend that two factors assure our inevitable success. The first is that we always draw to us exactly what we need at a given time, and the second is that the soul possesses a pattern of perfection within itself just waiting to be awakened by the human will. Ultimately, whether or not we awaken to that pattern of wholeness or learn the lesson in any given situation is dependent upon ourselves and whether or not we choose to follow through on doing the best that we know to do. Frequently, Cayce admonished individuals who asked what they were supposed to be doing in their lives: "That has been given over and over again, here in this: In *applying* that ye know *today!* and tomorrow the next step is given. For it is line upon line, precept upon precept, here a little, there a little" (826-11).

Throughout the years that individuals received readings, Edgar Cayce discussed a number of steps for creating soul mate relationships: (1) Learn to love and understand yourself; (2) Establish a spiritual ideal that can serve as a directional beacon; (3) Begin to work on and apply the best that you know to do; and (4) Expect things to change so that they can.

For some, learning to truly love and understand themselves is a difficult proposition. Perhaps because of upbringing, personal insecurities, self-esteem, or the negative influence of people around them, sometimes individuals feel as though they are not worthy to be loved or that they have little to share with others. Unfortunately, this negative imaging creates a pattern that is difficult to overcome because it feeds upon itself. Oftentimes, the individuals who have the lowest self-image are the very people who seem to be surrounded by such relationships as an overbearing parent, a demanding boss, a critical spouse, or an unmanageable child. In this situation, Cayce might tell the person that because "like attracts like," he or she is constantly drawing to him- or herself individuals who possess the same attitude that the person is holding as a self-image. The lesson is not necessarily to get rid of every relationship of this nature, but instead, to begin to cultivate personal regard, self-esteem, and self-love.

This "like attracts like" dynamic not only suggests that everything we put out through our thoughts and our deeds comes back to us, but also that we can see our own strengths and weaknesses in other people. Simply stated, individuals toward whom we have an emotional response literally act as a mirror. Cayce believed that the people in our life who may be the most frustrating to us are frustrating because we are seeing in them a portion of ourselves that we have somehow overlooked or refused to deal with. Conversely, the people in our life whom we truly admire are showing us a reflection of some quality we can utilize within ourselves. Although this concept might be difficult to believe, all one need do is to remember that even my own worst enemy has a best friend, and even my best friend has someone who doesn't like that person. Why? The answer has to do with the focus of our individual perceptions and our propensity to see in others the very thing we possess within ourselves.

The readings suggest that whenever we have an emotional response to another person (positive or negative) we can be certain that there is something more for us to learn. If we want to see what we need to work on spiritually, all we need do is look around at the people in our lives who drive us crazy. If we want to see what we have to work with, simply look around at the people whom we truly admire. In this manner, we will begin to see our own strengths and weaknesses portrayed in others. Becoming aware of this dynamic can give us an entirely different attitude about all of humankind. Cayce believed that as we come to know our true individuality, we would discover our connectedness with one another. We would also realize that with God as our Parent, we are all children of the same family.

From Cayce's perspective, the second important step in creating soul mate relationships is to establish a conscious ideal. In simplest terms, an ideal is a spiritual motivation or intent that becomes the basic foundation for why we do what we do. Once we establish an appropriate intent, we can create patterns of behavioral responses that are firmly based on a spiritual ideal rather than on our previous modes of behavior. Oftentimes, individuals have found that once they have continually experienced a certain type of challenging relationship with another person, it is difficult to change it. The reason is because a negative pattern has been created to such an extent that all they have to do is think about that person and they begin to feel the same levels of frustration and irritation within themselves—even when the person is nowhere around.

Cayce suggested that rather than continually *reacting to* previous experiences, establishing a conscious ideal enables an individual to *act on* a relationship, giving it the potential for a more positive direction. If, for example, an individual chose an ideal of forgiveness in a particular relationship, rather than reacting to a relationship challenge based upon old response patterns, the individual could instead ask questions such as: "How would a truly forgiving person respond in this situation?" "What is a forgiving person like?" "If I were a forgiving person, how would I behave?" Once an image of a forgiving person (or a loving person or an understanding person, etc.) has been established, then the challenge is simply to act accordingly. As an individual works with an ideal and establishes a new pattern, such as forgiveness, it takes the place of previous response patterns and eventually becomes automatic in the process.

The third step in creating soul mate relationships is the process of application. The simplicity of how this is accomplished is as follows: "For it is not in some great deed, not in some great form. But just being kind, being gentle, being patient, being longsuffering, showing brotherly love . . . " (793-2). The readings suggest that, for many individuals, too often there was a difference between knowledge and application. Cayce believed that unless something was applied, it could not become a part of personal awareness and therefore could not promote individual change. In other words, there is a vast difference between knowledge, which is simply information, and application, which can facilitate personal transformation.

The final step for transforming relationships is simply one of maintaining an attitude of openness and personal expectation. Cayce encouraged individuals to expect things to change so that they could. The readings were adamant that all relationships could be healed because ultimately the only individual one could change was oneself. As individuals changed themselves, the dynamic of "like attracts like" would inevitably transform the ways in which others responded. In other words, we most effectively heal our relationships with others by becoming whole within ourselves. Aspects of these steps for creating soul mate relationships can be found in many of the case histories contained in the Cayce archives.

In 1941 a newlywed couple came to Edgar Cayce seeking advice for living and growing together successfully. Told that they had been together previously, Cayce suggested that they had the ability to become true complements to one another. At the same time, however, they needed to remember that there would definitely be arguments during the course of their relationship. Cayce advised the couple, "Do not both get angry at the same time." In order to work together, they were encouraged to find ideals and purposes upon which they could both agree: "Their manner of approach, their manner of thought need not necessarily be the same, but the purpose, the desire, the hopes, the welfare of each should be as is indicated in such a union, one for the other" (341-48). Finally, they were encouraged to become a "helpmeet" toward one another, always attempting to place the other's welfare before their own.

A twenty-year-old woman was concerned that there would be difficulties because of her and her fiancé's different religious backgrounds and families. Cayce told her, "Remember, ye are marrying one man, *not* a family, *not* a church!" As long as she and her husband-to-be placed their relationship above that of the family and truly attempted to follow God's will for their lives, they would not have a problem. In addition to minimizing one another's faults and magnifying each other's virtues, the couple was reminded: "*Know* that thy associations are to be on a fifty-fifty basis, not forty-sixty nor twenty-eighty but *fifty-fifty!* and that ye must adjust thyselves to each *other's* idiosyncrasies or peculiarities" (1722-1). The reading promised that as they truly worked with each other and created a beautiful, joyful, worthwhile, and spiritual life together, those around them would be prompted to do likewise.

A thirty-one-year-old woman, experiencing a number of relationship challenges with family members and associates, was encouraged to keep in mind that whatever she desired to receive from others she should attempt to give them first. She was also advised that the faults she was seeing in others were a reflection of her own and that she alone possessed the ability to make positive changes in all of her relationships. In terms of holding the appropriate attitude and sense of expectancy in mind, her reading stated: "*Do not* hold the idea, 'Well, I know what they are going to say or do, but I'll do as best I can.' Disregard that! *Know* the spirit with which *ye* do a thing is the spirit that will respond to thee!" (1688-9).

In a contemporary story of relationships, Joe and Christine acknowledge that in terms of creating a soul mate relationship in marriage, they are "finally getting it right." Together for the past six years, this is the third marriage for each. Although Joe has come to the conclusion that his previous spouses were also soul mates, it is only since he's been with Christine that he believes he has changed enough in order to finally be in a healthy relationship. In discussing his previous marriages, Joe states that his other marriages each spanned more than fifteen years in duration. Both marriages had times that were very good as well as times that were very bad:

> We stayed through many difficult and emotional times. We learned to hate, to forgive, and then to hate some more. Finally, both marriages turned to indifference on all levels—not at all healthy. We fought over everything. We became involved in satisfying whatever desire crawled out of us. By the grace of God we moved on but with each relationship I was pushed higher to find some answers and to discover a purer purpose for living.

In the present, Christine and Joe think that their friendship and their interest in spirituality are the two greatest stabilizing influences in their lives. Convinced of their ongoing connection with one another, they obtained psychic readings which placed them together in Italy as brother and sister and as a couple working with healing at the time of Jesus. In this life, they also knew one another for more than thirteen years as friends while each was involved with other marriages. For both of them, their present relationship continues to be a learning experience. According to Christine:

> I've probably learned more from Joe than from anyone else . . . the thing that comes to mind first is that I've learned to become a better person by be-

ing with him. I used to have a mean streak in that I wanted to get revenge when I was hurt. Since I met Joe, however, he has been my conscience. Through him I've definitely become a better person. He also introduced me to the Edgar Cayce material and a whole new way of viewing life. I don't know that I've actually taught him anything, but he has made the statement that he feels as if he's meeting himself.

In discussing one of the problems that they worked through together, Christine tells the story of her son from a previous marriage who was living with his father. The problem was with her ex-husband. Although she communicated with her son, she didn't want anything to do with the former husband. Over a period of time she had a number of dreams that seemed to suggest she really needed to communicate with him and work on forgiveness. In spite of Joe's encouragement to do just that, Christine stubbornly refused to have anything to do with him. When a lawyer's letter stated that her "ex" wanted to change her visitation rights and sue *her* for child support, she became even angrier. He made quite a bit more money than she did and the whole idea was preposterous. Still, Joe tried to get his wife to work out the agreement with her "ex" before the courts stepped in, but she wouldn't deal with the situation.

Finally, the case went to court. Even the lawyer for Christine's "ex" was shocked when the judge ruled in favor of the ex-husband. Christine was ordered to pay child support! Although it was difficult for Christine to understand the situation, Joe convinced her that they could see it as part of the healing process. Over the next nine months, Christine worked with prayer for herself and her ex-husband, and Joe encouraged the two of them to begin opening up the lines of communication. When the time finally came for a court discussion about her son's college expenses, Christine and her ex-husband had worked out the situation even before their meeting with the attorneys and, according to Joe, went away from the proceedings with a smile and a new feeling about one another. Ever since that time, Christine and her "ex" have tried to be cooperative.

In terms of what Joe thinks he has gotten from his wife, he acknowledges that because of their personal growth, they have more similarities than differences. Perhaps their greatest difference is that Joe tends to be the emotional partner whereas Christine has an almost left-brained approach to everything. However, they've learned to be a complement to each other's emotional makeup. Most importantly, Joe thinks that Christine has been extremely helpful in enabling him to come to know himself:

> Christine has taught me more about myself in the last six years than I learned in the previous forty-eight because I finally see myself as I really am, especially those annoying little things we place so much importance on in our relationships. Sometimes it's really a hurting glance at myself, but it also makes me appreciate her all the more since she is so willing to be my mirror. Christine says I have helped her handle difficult situations and people by trying to look at the good that can come from those situations . . . For me, our being best friends has remained our constant over time.

In 1939 Edgar Cayce reminded a twenty-one-year-old plumber that it was not by chance that he had come into the earth or that he had cultivated relationships with his friends and associates, but rather as a means of personal transformation and growth by having had those experiences and relationships (2030-1). As to how he could

begin working with his relationships, he was told to discover ways in which he could make all of his interactions
with others a *"beautiful experience."* He was also encouraged to constantly ask himself: "What may I do or be to
others, that they may be better, may have a greater concept of the purposes of life, by even being acquainted or
associated with myself?"

A thirty-five-year-old accountant wanted to know if—
as far as the universe was concerned—he owed the
members of his family anything, and if so, what? Cayce
stated that there was a duty and an obligation he owed
toward every member of his family, just as they owed it
to him. Ultimately, that obligation was to work on improving themselves and their relationships with one another, becoming better people for having had the
opportunity of being with one another. In terms of making this a reality, the man was reminded that there was
nothing stronger than the power of his own free will
(1432-1). Likewise, a twenty-four-year-old man was told
that within himself he had the abilities "to do much good
or to do much harm!" (633-2). Advised that he would
eventually meet himself in all of his activities with others, he was encouraged to become a constructive influence and to let peace, harmony, beauty, and love become
the ruling factors in his life.

Parents who wanted to know the best way to raise
their son, making his life happy and healthy, were told
that one of the most constructive things they could provide for their child was a spiritual foundation which
would remain with him throughout his life. In addition,
they were encouraged to be true to what they desired to
create in their son and "Never do anything ye would not
have him do. Never say anything ye would not have him
say" (1551-2).

The fact that creating soul mate relationships is an
essential purpose for being in the earth was clearly ex-

plained in 1938 to a sixty-seven-year-old man. During his reading, he was assured that he was on the right path and he was advised: "Be not weary in well-doing" (1598-1). He was told that ultimately there was only one ideal in human relationships and that was to "Love thy neighbor as thyself." When the man asked how he could be of greatest service to others, he was encouraged to give light to those who sat in darkness, to bring hope to those who had become discouraged, and to help those who had become lost to find their direction. If he did these things with the proper intent—not forcing his beliefs or thoughts upon others, but instead helping them find what was meaningful to them—he would enable others to find themselves as well as their relationship with the Creator.

A contemporary example of discovering more about oneself through personal relationships is illustrated in the story of Tim and Carl. Both men are thirty, gay, and have been together for the past three years. The couple have found that they have many similarities and differences between them, both of which have been ultimately helpful in personal growth. From Carl's perspective, the differences have enabled them to expand their individual perceptions of life. The positive similarities have been comforting, but similar negative patterns between them have sometimes been challenging. According to Carl, they are alike in many ways and still manage to complement one another:

> Being a same-sex love relationship, there may appear not to be the exchange of opposites, complements as the yin and yang, the masculine and the feminine energies, yet we find the complements exist on deeper levels than the physical. In some ways, our mental, emotional, and spiritual processes are quite different.

Their relationship includes a love of learning, spirituality, and heart-to-heart talks. By being together, Tim
thinks he has come to learn more about love—not only
love for another person, but also love for himself. In discussing their relationship, Tim says:

> Carl has been my "life line" at times when I have
> struggled to maintain my personal integrity. Some
> of his strongest personal attributes are the very
> ones I'm trying to develop within myself. For each
> other, we take turns being "the rock," "the sup-
> porter," and "the mirror" during our personal
> struggles. He reminds me of who and what I really
> am, and supports me whenever I falter and need to
> reach higher. At the same time, it's not so much
> what I've learned from Carl but what I've learned
> about myself from this relationship. I've been able
> to see myself more clearly. I've been able to see pat-
> terns that I have that I didn't like and to begin to
> change them. One of the biggest lessons I've begun
> to see is that I can open myself up more and more
> completely to another soul and not lose myself or
> my individuality. I can feel more complete and
> more powerful by following my personal fulfillment
> and, at the same time, be deeply interwoven with
> another person.

In 1943 Edgar Cayce told a forty-three-year-old woman
that she and her husband had picked up their marriage
relationship exactly where they had left it off from a previous lifetime in the Holy Land. Because they had never
agreed on anything at that time, they didn't agree in the
present. Cayce assured her that there were many things
they could do to become cooperative with one another.
In order to begin transforming their relationship, they
were encouraged to: "Work together! Find those things

# SEEKING INFORMATION ON

**holistic health, spirituality, dreams, intuition or ancient civilizations?**

**Call 1-800-723-1112, visit our Web site, or mail in this postage-paid card for a FREE catalog of books and membership information.**

Name: _____

Address: _____

City: _____

State/Province: _____

Postal/Zip Code: _____ Country: _____

Association for Research and Enlightenment, Inc.
215 67th Street
Virginia Beach, VA 23451-2061

**For faster service, call 1-800-723-1112.**
**www.edgarcayce.org**

PBIN

upon which you agree, stress them, rather than those on which ye disagree" (2792-3).

Another couple were encouraged to start seeing one another as a "complement" to themselves. To be sure, they were not wholly alike nor did they think alike, but they could grow and expand by being with one another (1100-31).

A twenty-three-year-old minister was encouraged to become a channel of blessings to others. He was told that as he pulled forth from himself the very best that he had to offer, he would act as a "leavening" influence to those around him. He was encouraged to condemn no one, neither himself nor others, and to keep himself "unspotted" from the cares of the world. As he attempted to do all of these things, the glory of the Creator could become manifest in the earth through him (3188-1).

A woman who was experiencing difficult relationships in her life with various family members and associates was encouraged to keep working at healing the problems: "Do not expect results in one day, nor one week. Individuals do not sow one day and reap the next. They reap what they have sown in the periods when *that* sown has come to fruitage. For what ye sow, so shall ye reap" (971-1). She was advised that as long as she kept trying to do the right thing in the right spirit, with gentleness, kindness, and patience, success would inevitably come to her.

A Cayce reading told a forty-six-year old woman that ultimately the soul only kept what it gave away. With that in mind, she needed to become mindful of the way she treated others because whatever patience she attempted to work with, whatever the extent of her love, her kindness, and her gentleness, all these things were exactly what she would receive in return (5259-1). Another woman was advised that her relationship with her mother had become strained and difficult because the

two had so frequently misinterpreted and misunderstood each other. The two were encouraged to set their
disagreements aside and to begin cultivating their relationship anew, discovering those things they had in
common as well as where they agreed (2706-1).

A very successful account of two individuals learning
to work together is portrayed in the story of Wayne and
Ruth, who have been married for nearly fifty years. Together they have raised two daughters; shared a lifetime
of occupations, experiences, and travel; and are seen by
outsiders as being completely attached to one another.
Their life journey has taken them through a thirty-year
career in the navy, a love of music, teaching, administra-
tive responsibilities with a nonprofit organization, and
even a two-year stint living on a sailboat. However, their
relationship did not start off easy.

Although they had an instant attraction when they
met, Wayne was more introverted, shied away from social contacts, and seemed very focused on his love of
music. Ruth, on the other hand, had broader interests, a
desire to be with people, and was much more extro-
verted. In spite of their differing backgrounds and personalities, the two married one year after meeting.
According to Ruth, "during much of our six-month engagement and during the first five years of our marriage,
we were frequently in heated arguments and said ugly
things to one another." In addition to the arguments, one
of the first major challenges came when Wayne's mother
kept actively trying to break up the marriage.

In the beginning, the couple's mode of behavior was
also quite different. Wayne was extremely slow and de-
liberate in all that he did. He was an absolute perfection-
ist and often insisted on finishing something even when
there was no longer a reason for doing so. Conversely,
Ruth was too quick to come to conclusions and then to
act on them. According to Ruth, in the face of all these

differences, the couple came to the conclusion that "we either had to learn to get along or to part company." The couple began talking things out rather than arguing with one another.

Wayne came to realize that he had to decide which was more important: his relationship with his mother or his relationship with his wife. He chose his marriage. The couple also realized that they could learn from one another, and they each began to modify their behavioral extremes. Today, Ruth and Wayne are convinced that they have become better people for having had the opportunity to work together.

Over time, the couple's communication improved to such an extent that both of their daughters tell the story of frequently falling asleep to the sound of their parents' voices "chatting" through the bedroom walls only to awaken to the same sound the next morning. Even now, the couple find that they enjoy each other's company and sharing the things that they have in common:

> We share a strong interest in things spiritual, in the beauty of nature, in the British Isles, the Orient, and biblical history. We also enjoy gardening and woodworking. I love to hear Wayne play his clarinet and he still enjoys my ability to organize.

Ruth believes that soul mate relationships are those which have occurred over many lifetimes in various types of relationships. She states, "They help each other work with karmic patterns. Hopefully, this is done mostly in a supportive way." Tying in with their career in the navy and their love of sailing, they have had past-life experiences when they were brothers working together on a large sailing ship and when they were husband and wife in a fishing village off the Brittany coast during the fourteenth century.

Demonstrating their connection and deep love for one another, after thirty years of travel and transfers because of his navy career, when Wayne retired, he told Ruth, "You've followed me for the last thirty years, for the next thirty it's my turn to follow you." That promise has led them through two years in the Bahamas, a dedication to working with spirituality and personal transformation groups, and finally to their latest career as bed and breakfast innkeepers. Ruth smiles and says, "For the last forty-three-and-a-half years we have worked at being supportive to each other in all ways."

Echoing the fact that soul mate relationships are created over time, the readings told a twenty-eight-year-old lawyer contemplating marriage that happiness was not so much a thing that existed, but instead was a state of experience that could be created. Cayce advised the couple that should they decide to marry, they were to live so that they could always depend upon one another. They were also encouraged to conduct themselves so that they would never let themselves down in terms of their personal behavior. Living in this manner while maintaining the proper attitudes and spiritual focus in their lives, the couple would inevitably have happiness, peace, and contentment in their marriage (939-1).

A husband who came to Edgar Cayce for a reading stated that his relationship with his wife was less than desirable. He complained that there was very little that the two shared in common. If only for the sake of the children, he wanted to know how they could begin working together, experiencing more love and good will between them. Cayce asked the man, "Have ye considered what sort of man you would like to have if ye were in your wife's shoes?" He was encouraged to begin acting just like that type of a husband and, as a result, the couple's relationship would change (3411-1).

A twenty-year-old artist wanted to know whether she

should discontinue the relationship she had with a very challenging friend. Cayce encouraged her to keep working at it because no individual had too many friends and each relationship was important in itself (1828-1). Another individual was told that the best way to start healing any relationship was simply to begin minimizing the other person's faults and to magnify his or her virtues (2925-1).

A man seeking harmony in his family was told that instead of trying to have his own way or attempting to bring others around to his way of thinking, the only person he could change was himself. He was encouraged to seek harmony within himself, to stop trying to change others, and to stop blaming them for events in his life. His family life was out of harmony because *he* was out of harmony. If he effected the changes he sought within himself, his family relationships would be healed in turn (4733-1).

A thirty-six-year-old woman seeking marital advice was told that rather than trying to change her husband by her own will or personal contention, she should act in the same manner toward him that she wished him to act in return. When she wanted to know how to bring her understanding of spiritual truths to her husband, it was suggested that rather than constantly trying to tell him about those truths, she would do much better by showing him by her example. When she inquired how they could handle challenges that arose in their relationship, such as finances, she was encouraged to find ways to discuss the problem "not in anger, not in wrath," but in ways that would enable them to solve their joint challenges and obligations together (585-1).

In a final example from the Edgar Cayce readings, a twenty-three-year-old woman sought advice about her upcoming marriage. In beginning the reading, Cayce stated that his desire was to provide information that would be "the most helpful in the soul and development mentally of each" (480-20). The reading stated that the couple had the ability to complement one another, but unless they remembered that marriage was a "fifty-fifty proposition," they could end up being at odds.

The woman was told that she had the natural tendency to be the leader and the greater influence in their marriage. She was encouraged to become mindful of this fact so that she never overshadowed the abilities or the activities of her husband in any way. Rather than becoming subservient to one another, the two were encouraged to share, as equals, the best that they had within themselves.

In their disagreements, the couple was advised to never "rail" at one another or to become angry but to rather "always *reason* well together." They were encouraged to become as interested in their partner's activities as they were in their own in their social time. Although it was fine to have differing interests and activities, the two were encouraged to cooperate with one another at every possible occasion. They were told to budget their time so that there was time for each other, for work, for recreation, and for recuperation. In all these endeavors they were told to be cooperative with one another. As they worked together, their marriage would be a helpful experience for each and the "crowning influence" in their lives.

Ideally, their home was to become the earthly shadow of a "heavenly home," a place "where an angel would *desire* to visit, where an angel would seek to be a guest." It wasn't simply to be a place to rest or to sleep or to eat, but a place where every individual who entered could feel a sense of sacredness, a sense of helpfulness, and a sense of hopefulness in the very energy of their home. In terms of creating harmony in their marriage, they were advised not to think, "We will do it tomorrow—we will begin next week—we will make for such next year." Instead, it was suggested that they work with each other every day, building toward a more perfect union. Whenever they had doubts or fears, they were to work with one another and to take their concerns into meditation and prayer where their Creator could help them. As they followed these suggestions, their marriage would be blessed and fruitful and they could be used as channels of God's love in the earth.

Throughout the years he gave readings, Cayce advised individuals that it wasn't so important *what* they were in life but rather *who* they were in the process of becoming by having the opportunity to be with all the other people in their life. In the soul's search for personal wholeness, he believed that soul mate relationships were possible and even inevitable with every human being that we come in contact. The challenge is that some of these relationships call us to undergo personal change and transformation through a sometime difficult process of personal application. And yet, Cayce assured individuals that regardless of the nature of their present relationship, personal healing could take place. Apparently, each one of us is called to transform that corner of the world in which we find ourselves, healing one relationship at a time:

And unless each soul entity (and this entity especially) makes the world better, that corner or place of the world a little better, a little bit more hopeful, a little bit more patient, showing a little more of brotherly love, a little more of kindness, a little more of longsuffering—by the very words and deeds of the entity, the life is a failure; especially so far as growth is concerned. Though you gain the whole world, how little ye must think of thyself if ye lose the purpose for which the soul entered this particular sojourn! 3420-1

# 11

## Our Soul Mate Relationship with the Creator

They are not of the world, even as I am not of the world
. . . That they all may be one; as thou, Father, art in me,
and I in thee, that they also may be one in us: that the
world may believe that thou hast sent me.

And the glory which thou gavest me I have given
them; that they may be one, even as we are one . . .

Jesus of Nazareth
The Gospel of John (17:16, 21-22)

From the perspective of the Edgar Cayce readings, there is a common bond that unites all of humanity. Simply stated, that bond results from the fact that there is only one God and each soul is one of His children. For this reason, it is sadly ironic that religion, the very structure intended to enrich our relationship with God, is oftentimes the one thing that divides us most as a human family. As a result, many individuals have given up their faith in God because of their disillusionment with humankind. In order to address this problem, the readings, rather than focusing upon the forms of specific religions or dogmas, focus on the importance of every single soul learning to manifest an awareness of the living spirit in the earth. In response to a question regarding religious orthodoxy, Cayce stated:

> . . . what is the difference . . . Truth . . . is of the One source. Are there not trees of oak, of ash, of pine? There are the needs of these for meeting this or that experience . . .
>
> Then, all will fill their place. Find not fault with *any*, but rather show forth as to just how good a pine, or ash, or oak, or *vine* thou art! 254-87

Along these same lines, Cayce told a thirty-three-year-old Jewish stockbroker that because the Creator was the source of all that existed, the first lesson in any spiritual journey should be "*One*—One—One—*One*; Oneness of God, oneness of man's relation, oneness of force, oneness of time, oneness of purpose, *oneness* in every effort—Oneness—Oneness!" (900-429). However, to the same person the readings also acknowledged that it might be as hard for some individuals to understand this reality of oneness as it would be to explain third-dimensional reality to a two-dimensional being. It was a personal experience that an individual would grow into only as the soul grew and evolved.

In 1941 a writer asked Edgar Cayce why God had decided to create souls in the first place. The answer was that it was out of His desire to seek expression and to have companionship (5749-14). Although the idea of the Creator needing companionship might sound surprising at first, it makes sense when one considers the fact that the nature of God is love. Frequently, Cayce stated that love was best expressed as the giving out of oneself with no thought of receiving in return. From this perspective, then, love can only be manifested through the process of *having relationships with others.* For its own part, the soul finds itself in a physical body in an attempt to experience the dynamics of cause and effect, eventually learning to manifest perfect love, and, in time, becoming a fit companion for the Creator.

Frequently, the Edgar Cayce readings reminded individuals of their basic spiritual essence. From Cayce's perspective, each individual was not a physical body, but rather a spiritual being—created in the image of an all-loving Creator—who was having a physical experience in the earth. In other words, the soul may undergo a series of physical lifetimes, but it is much more than simply a body. Just as is stated in scripture, the soul was created in "God's image" (Genesis 1:26) and therefore its natural state is spirit. In the process of Creation, God gave to each soul complete freedom of choice and the opportunity to find self-expression.

For these reasons, the nature of each soul is that of a "seeker"—seeking its true identity and its relationship to the whole. Unfortunately, we may spend a lifetime searching and not ever realize what it is we are actually looking for; ultimately from Cayce's perspective, it is simply our relationship with the Creator. The essential question repeatedly posed by the soul might be *"Who Am I?"* This question is addressed in infinite ways as each soul chooses specific experiences to meet itself. Once this process was complete, Cayce believed that all souls would eventually reawaken to their individuality and their true companionship with God.

Cayce told a thirty-seven-year-old schoolteacher in 1935 that what she was being called to do as a soul in the earth was not all that difficult: "Just being kind, just being patient, just showing love for thy fellow man." By consistently living in such a manner, she would become a channel for bringing spirit into the earth. In time, she would reawaken to that portion of herself which was a child of the Creator. Cayce promised, "The soul, then, must return—*will* return—to its Maker. It is a portion of the Creative Force, which is energized into activity even in materiality, in the flesh" (272-9).

Another woman was reminded that the ultimate purpose in life for every single soul was simply so that the individual could reawaken to the truth of its spiritual essence, becoming a "fit companion" for the Creator in the process. She was advised that whenever she found herself asking, "Why—*why*—have I come into this experience?" she was to look for those individuals who had been sent into her life for the purpose of enabling her to express love and service. As she worked with those around her joyfully, they would become the means of helping her find herself.

> Not in selfishness, not in grudge, not in wrath; not in *any* of those things that make for the separation of the I AM from the Creative Forces, or Energy, or God. But the simpleness, the gentleness, the humbleness, the faithfulness, the long-suffering, *patience!* These be the attributes and those things which the soul takes cognizance of in its walks and activities before men. 518-2

With this thought in mind, a seventy-six-year-old manufacturer was told that whether or not a soul developed or regressed in any given lifetime was dependent upon how well that soul applied itself in love and service to others (1767-2).

A fifty-one-year-old housewife and mother inquired how she could best guide and direct her twenty-eight-year-old son, who was having problems. She was encouraged to place love and support above control and having her own way: "in *loving* tolerance, in loving association, ever being ready to answer when any aid or help must be given or may be given" (255-12). Although she could love her son and give him advice and counsel, she could not live his life for him. Cayce reminded her that, ultimately, on its own, "each soul must find its way back to its God."

A fifty-one-year-old governess was told that the "whole law" was expressed simply as follows, "Love the Lord with all thy heart, thy mind, thy body; thy neighbor as thyself" (1250-1). In the same manner, a twenty-seven-year-old writer was advised that the life of Jesus had served as a pattern for all human beings regardless of their religious affiliation. From this perspective, Jesus was an "Elder Brother" for every soul in the earth. When the man asked how he could start living in accord with this pattern, Cayce suggested:

> Not in mighty deeds of valor, not in the exaltation of thy knowledge or thy power; but in the gentleness of the things of the spirit: Love, kindness, long-suffering, patience; these thy brother hath shown thee that thou, applying them in thy associations with thy fellow man day by day, here a little, there a little, may become one with Him as He has *destined* that thou shouldst be! Wilt thou separate thyself? For there be nothing in heaven, in earth, in hell, that may separate thee from the love of thy God, of thy brother, save thine own self! 849-11

Elsewhere, this pattern of behavior which was the heritage of every soul was described as "the awareness within each soul, imprinted in pattern on the mind and waiting to be awakened by the will, of the soul's oneness with God" (5749-14).

A sixty-one-year-old widow seeking direction in life was told that as a child of God she possessed a portion of

His consciousness and her life should be for the purpose of attempting to manifest the Creator's love. Gradually, she would become aware of her spiritual source as she lived in accord with the best that she knew to do, "here a little, there a little, line upon line, precept upon precept" (3003-1).

A thirty-seven-year-old woman who sought companionship and marriage in an effort to feel a sense of personal wholeness was advised, "know, the soul is rather the soul-mate of the universal consciousness than of an individual entity" (2988-2). With this same thought in mind, a group of people working with the Cayce information were told, "for He is *lonely* without thee" (254-76). They were encouraged to find ways in which they could be of service to those around them, and to learn to love one another "even as He has loved you."

The call that we should begin loving one another as the Creator loves us is not at all surprising if we are His children. The readings suggest that our growth in awareness will only be possible as we reach out to one another in this fashion:

> Then, as there has been and is the passage of a soul through time and space, through this and that experience, it has been and is for the purpose of giving more and more opportunities to express that which justifies man in his relationships one with another; in mercy, love, patience, long-suffering, brotherly love. 938-1

At the very least, the fact that we are children of an all-loving Creator should leave us with a sense of awesome responsibility. Quite simply, that responsibility is to learn to love one another. The question of how effectively that goal was being realized was perhaps best expressed to a group in 1932 when Cayce asked them,

" . . . art *thou* ready to give account of that *thou* hast done with thine opportunity in the earth as the Sons of God . . . ?" (364-7).

Without a doubt, the entire world would become transformed if every individual suddenly came to the realization that the ultimate purpose for being alive was simply to learn how to love. Rather than being a philosophical possibility, Cayce was confident that, in time, every soul would come to an awareness of that very realization. An awareness that would enable each soul to find its personal wholeness and to come to an understanding that since we have been integrally and inextricably connected to the Creator since the dawn of our Creation, we are soul mates with Him.

# Epilogue

As long as there have been human beings, there have been individuals who have felt prompted to search for something missing in their lives, all the while hoping they can find it in another person. This idealized view of human relationships has oftentimes been described as looking for one's "other half," a "twin soul," or a "soul mate." Many have come to believe that a soul mate relationship is a perfect partnership that will somehow make their life complete—an idea popularized by contemporary society. Although Edgar Cayce definitely agreed with the idea that individuals had soul mates, his perspective was entirely different and ultimately more helpful.

Rather than thinking that the soul mate condition was a perfect relationship that exists between two people, Cayce believed that these relationships were an ongoing learning, growing, and experiential process. Perfect relationships were not simply found; they had to be created. Although some individuals might appear to have the ideal relationship in the present, the Cayce information suggests that these types of relationships have evolved over time as two individuals have learned to work together. Too often, individuals have left a challenging relationship in pursuit of a supposed "soul mate" only to discover that challenges and difficulties arose in the new relationship as well. Most often, other individuals are not the cause of our problems; they simply enable us to encounter the very lessons we need for soul growth and personal transformation.

For decades Cayce provided thousands of individuals with practical and helpful advice for creating soul mate relationships in their own lives. Regardless of whether a relationship was between a couple, between friends, among family members, or between two individuals who were simply having difficulties, Cayce believed that the ultimate purpose of our associations with one another is to help us stretch and change and grow. Ideally, through the process of having relationships, individuals would help one another become better people for having had the opportunity of being together.

Because of his clairvoyant talents, Cayce had the ability to view the development of relationships over time and describe how past-life relationships and influences affect the present. A soul mate relationship is an ongoing connection with another individual that the soul picks up again in various times and places. That connection enables both individuals to come to know themselves and to grow in their awareness of their relationship with the Creator. The soul mate condition is not just contained within sexual relationships; it also exists among parents and children, friends and family, even work associates. For this reason, each individual has many soul mates to help her or him in this process of personal growth. To be sure, soul mate relationships are purposeful, but they are simply regular relationships among people who possess an extraordinary connection.

Frequently Cayce called relationships "a fifty-fifty proposition," in which the important question became not "What am I going to get out of this?" but rather "What is the very best that I can put into it?" With this in mind, the Cayce readings suggest that true love is not really passion, or desire, or even affection; instead, it is the self-less act of giving out the very best that one has within oneself. Although they are not always easy, all relationships have the opportunity to become a purposeful experience. As to whether or not individuals experience their personal relationships "for weal or for woe" ultimately depends upon their manner of application. In countless situations Cayce reminded individuals that the capacity to make personal change was within themselves. In spite of the fact that past-life experiences can create probabilities and potentials, it is what individuals do with their free will in the present that shapes the course of their lives.

Through an ongoing process of relationships, experiences, and various lifetimes, the soul finds itself involved in a curriculum of personal growth and development. Because we are children of an all-loving Creator, Cayce believed that learning how to love other people is what we're here to learn—eventually all souls become soul mates with one another. In fact, the more a soul becomes whole, the more able it is to connect with other people. Individuals are attracted to one another at a soul level not because they are each others' unique complement, but by being together each can provide the other with the impetus to become whole. From this perspective, the story of soul mates is really the story of the soul's individual search for wholeness. However, true wholeness can only be accomplished as the soul reawakens to its spiritual source. For this reason, ultimately, our search for soul mates is our search for God.

# A.R.E. PRESS